HOW TO PLAY
MADISON SQUARE
GARDEN

WHAT OTHERS ARE SAYING ABOUT
HOW TO PLAY MADISON SQUARE GARDEN

"Many 'how to' books are written by pretenders. Mindi not only inarguably knows the subject, but has also delivered her "user manual" in a clear and concise style, benefitting readers at every level of career development. Her logical analysis of a performer's obligation to connect with their audience shouldn't be ignored! Anyone absorbing the Nascar analogy will absolutely smoke the competition; just like Mindi does every time she takes the stage.

> —**Jim Ed Norman,** former President Warner/Reprise Nashville, arranger for the Eagles; producer for Anne Murray, Hank Williams Jr.

"To me the writing and recording of a song is only the tip of the rock 'n' roll iceberg—the performance of that song is really what makes the connection with the audience and creates hits. When your intent on stage is to convince, connect, and communicate, you will dominate, and the rush the audience feels will result in a standing "O" every time. We as performers are at the control panel to make that happen. This book will show you the way."

> —**Jim Peterik**, co-founder of The Ides of March and Survivor. Writer of "Eye Of The Tiger," "Vehicle," and 18 top 20 hits. Author of "Songwriting For Dummies" and veteran of Madison Square Garden

"If you have the talent, there is no excuse for failure in today's music business, just as long as you work hard enough. The trouble is, most artists don't know what they need to work on. There's usually a missing piece of the puzzle. And for success, the jigsaw must be complete. Read Mindi Abair's stunning "How To Play Madison Square Garden" and you'll have all those elusive little nuggets of success right at your fingertips. The bottom line is, how much do you really want to succeed? If you need it bad, get this book. It'll be the best career move you've made this year!"

    —Chris Standring, Producer, Recording Artist, & CEO of A&R Online

"Great read! Mindi captures the essence for triumph in this business. Be true to yourself in every aspect of your perform-ance. Establish yourself in front of your audience and deliver the "message" with confidence and sincerity. Mastering the art of performance is a definite path for overall success!"

    —Mark Wexler, Senior Vice President Label Manager-Jazz & Classics Concord Music Group

"In the beginning we could barely play our own songs—awkwardly squeaking out vocal melodies and fumbling through guitar chords—but having the confidence that comes with knowing how to perform worked magic for us and went a long way toward making the audience think we were better than we actually were. It gave us time to develop our musicianship and songwriting to match our stage show. It's an invaluable tool to know how to 'fake it' until you 'make it'."

    —Luke Smith, Brite Futures

"If anyone knows what it takes to not only give an audience a memorable performance, but actually take them places they weren't expecting, it's Mindi. She is a performer's performer and anyone coming up the ranks would do themselves a great service by taking notes at her live shows and reading her book."

    —Matthew Hager, Multi-platinum producer and song-writer

HOW TO PLAY
MADISON SQUARE
GARDEN

Mindi Abair, Lance Abair and Ross Cooper

How To Play Madison Square Garden
Mindi Abair, Lance Abair and Ross Cooper

Published by:
Not More Saxophone Music, Ink
www.howtoplaymadisonsquaregarden.com

ISBN-10: 0983936307
ISBN-13: 978-0-9839363-0-5

1. Entertainment 2. Music 3. Business 4. Performance

Front Cover Art: Patty Palazzo www.punkmasters.com
Book Interior Design: Karrie Ross www.KarrieRoss.com
Editor: Linda Abair
Illustrations by: Jeff Cooper

Printed in the United States of America

ACKNOWLEDGEMENTS

We would like to thank Lowell and Barbara Lytle and Young American Showcase for giving us a place to learn, grow and refine our knowledge of what it takes to be an excellent performer.

Thank you to all the past members of Young American Showcase, as you were the first students of the entertainment concepts taught in this book.

Thank you to every club owner, contractor and artist who hired me to play at their club or in their band. I was able to develop who I was on stage and how to convey that knowledge to others because of all these different experiences along the way. Dr. Lawrence Smith and Scott Straw, thanks for your thoughts and wisdom as we were starting to compile what we knew on paper. Patty Pallazzo, you created the coolest book cover I could have ever imagined. Jeff Cooper, thanks for all the illustrations. This book couldn't have happened without you.

To Linda Abair and Jason Steele, thanks for dealing with all the late nights and dinner table conversations about this book and the concepts included. We can move on and talk about something else at dinner from now on!

And to all the entertainers we have seen who have inspired us over the years, we thank you.

TABLE OF CONTENTS:

The music industry is changing rapidly, and along with that, so is the model for building a successful career. Year after year, less and less physical CDs are being sold. Meanwhile, more and more music is being made available digitally. Currently, the digital music revenue stream hasn't caught up to the money made from physical sales of CDs that are being lost every year. And it won't.

So where does this leave you as an artist? What is the new model for success? Make great music, create your own brand as an artist or band, and develop your skills as a live performer. Live performance is one of the strongest and most effective ways you can brand yourself. Branding is how people in today's music industry are turning their music into cash. Movie "X" wants your music in their movie because you embody what they want to portray in the movie. They want your brand. How do they know this? They've seen you perform. They've experienced your stage presence, attitude and energy on stage. Microsoft paid millions to use "Start Me Up" by the Rolling Stones. Why? They wanted the credibility and image that they could lend the Microsoft brand. It was literally worth millions of dollars to Microsoft.

The first and best way to create your brand and ensure a long and successful career is to become a great live performer. At this point in the music industry's history, it is your best chance for survival. Create a great live show and they will come. Everyone is able to post their music online. Everyone has their own website, YouTube channel, facebook and twitter pages. How do you cut through the millions of other musicians and bands that are out there and get heard and have a chance at greatness? Become a great live act. Become a great performer.

Do you remember your first concert? For most, it was a life-changing experience. When I heard Prince's music for the first time, I was a fan. But when I saw him live for the first time, I was a lifetime fan and I know everyone in the audience that night felt the same way. The same holds true for Bruce Springsteen. He's had a lot of hits, but much of his success has been based on what an explosive live performer he is and how hard his band works on stage every night. He's a blue collar musician, winning people over one at a time every single performance. He's built a following of millions that way.

Do you want to change people's lives and create fans for life every night? You hold that power in your hand. You can show people who you are, what you stand for, what you care about, and why they'll love you, in one evening. Then they'll want to be a part of your "brand." They'll buy your t-shirt. They'll buy your music. They'll eagerly follow you to the next concert and buy a ticket and tell their friends to buy a ticket. That's what you're building toward. That's what creates a lasting and meaningful career.

INTRODUCTION

Have you ever seen a multi-platinum artist and thought to yourself that they had little or no talent? In the same breath, have you ever seen an unknown, but very talented musician or singer and wondered why they aren't incredibly successful?

MUSIC EDUCATION DOESN'T INCLUDE ENTERTAINMENT CONCEPTS

In the vast majority of music schools, a person has a choice of many degree programs: Composition, conducting, songwriting, education, music history, music therapy, the business of music, and many others. There are courses in music theory, counterpoint, composition, performance, etc.

Since music has historically been considered a performing art, it is unfortunate that few of the major music schools offer training in not only how to <u>play</u>, but also how to <u>perform</u> music in front of an audience. They can teach you the tools of music theory and technique, but they omit tools that can make a significant impact on your ability to be consistently successful in front of a live audience. They typically omit teaching "**Entertainment Concepts.**" That's what you're going to learn in this book.

AUDIENCES HEAR WITH THEIR EYES

Most audience members have not graduated from a music school and thus have no idea whether you are a good musician or even playing in tune. In fact, many people typically describe a great performance by a band or singer by saying, "It's one of the best performances they've ever **seen**." With this in mind, it is important that the audience witness a performance that also **looks** successful and fun.

Today's generation has witnessed amazing performers such as Lady Gaga, Garth Brooks, Beyonce, Bruce Springsteen, Prince, and many more. We are now the "MTV, YouTube, Hyper-Media Generation," and being a proficient musician or songwriter just isn't enough. Audiences have become a lot more visually oriented, and therefore demand more from stage performers.

Take the cue, don't just sit there uploading your music to iTunes hoping the world will find you, or hoping your new video will go viral on YouTube. Create your destiny. Work toward becoming a great performer. Delve into what it takes to capture and maintain an audience's attention. Learn to draw them into your world and develop a relationship with them that will last a lifetime.

THE "QUALITY OF EXPERIENCE"

Many performers have had years of experience as musicians or studio musicians but still don't exhibit the professional polish and expertise it takes to win over an audience every time. While some musicians seem to be "born entertainers." How can you become one of the "born entertainers" even if you weren't born that way? There are tried and true methods to communicate with an audience and learn to become the performer you know you can be.

Study and emulate great entertainers. As a young child, Michael Jackson said he copied Fred Astaire's moves for months, and also spent hours in front of the television copying James Brown's moves. Michael Jackson went on to become one of the world's most famous and successful performers. He had hit songs, but he sold those hit songs night after night to live audiences all around the world. He made you believe what he was singing. He brought you into his world and made you feel what he was feeling. He wasn't born with that gift. He had incredible talent to start with, but he worked hard to become a breathtaking performer that could catapult his own talent to a whole new level. He knew exactly what he was doing when he lifted his arms into the air and screamed at the same place in the song every night. He calculated every step and every action he made toward every audience. He was a trained professional. And you can learn exactly what he knew by learning specific entertainment concepts and practicing them until you own them.

It's not the length of your experience or the magnitude of your talent that matters as much as the quality of your experience and learning. Entertainment concepts can be learned and honed. You can bring your music to the next level by creating ways to effectively share it with an audience. It will take time and thought and action on your part. You've spent years to learn your instrument or craft. It's time to take it to the next level.

Where can you practice what you're learning? There are many kinds of music and entertainment venues in which one can perform. There are recital halls, high school auditoriums, concert halls, garages, coffee shops, rock clubs, churches, cocktail lounges, Las Vegas showrooms, television programs, music festivals of all types, theaters, sports arenas, stadiums, state fairs and when all else fails, even the street. One of my first gigs was in the men's underwear section at Macy's department store. Trust me when I say that you can play and practice learning how to interact with an audience ANYWHERE. And that's what you need to think of it as... practice and experience.

Ask Dave Chapelle how much he learned by doing his stand up act on the street in Santa Monica for years. He built his persona there, and then made a fortune bringing it to the masses for television.

Each venue, along with its audience, places different demands for excellence on the musician/performer. Obviously, a young child's piano recital will have a very forgiving audience, while Madison Square Garden will have an audience that expects the highest degree of entertainment prowess. Take control of your destiny and create greatness every time you perform. The rest will follow.

But what if you are one of those people who have no choice but to play the smaller venues? Should you accept your lot in life and allow mediocrity to be your standard? Or, should you become a student of the art of entertainment and communication with the hopes of performing on a greater stage? Your practice in the smaller venues could well prepare you for a long and profitable career in the "big time." Have you heard the expression "It's not the destination, but the journey"? Use every night in a club to hone your skills. Go play on the street and learn to communicate with audience members who are two feet away from you crowding around. Become one with your instrument and your persona every night in a real world setting. Don't sit at home and just practice scales. Practice communication and interaction. Share what you're doing with the people around you at every chance you get. Learn to show an audience love and they will show you love back. Build your confidence and your performance skills. They'll move you to the next level faster than anything else.

A SUCCESS STORY

"Early in our career we won second place in a large battle-of-the-bands competition even though we could barely play our own songs. It was one of our first "major" shows in front of hundreds of people and esteemed real-life music industry judges. We took the stage with nothing more than a few keyboards, an iPod (no drummer), some spastic vocals, and a hell of a lot of confidence— the confidence that comes from knowing how to have fun and connect with an audience, knowing what they want to see, and not taking ourselves too seriously. We had played a lot of clubs and learned a lot about what works on stage. That confidence of knowing how to perform helped us beat out some very talented competition— a classically-trained jazz pianist and vocalist, and several strong, serious-minded rock bands— as well as win the "audience favorite" award by a landslide. Parents of some of the other bands were baffled (and they let us know it), but the audience and judges understood. They (the audience) were treated as friends and taken on a journey of undivided fun and love-reciprocation. These same "concepts" helped us get a manager, signed to a major label, slots on large-theater tours with big-name acts, and many, many exciting, successful live shows."

—Luke Smith, Brite Futures

You need every edge you can get in this ultra competitive business. Everyone wants to be a rock star. Most will never take the necessary steps or learn what it takes as a performer to get close. This book will give you the edge you need to become more than a songwriter, instrumentalist, singer, or just another band on stage. It will teach you how to interact with and win over an audience, and that can be priceless.

To quote a song from the Beatles "And in the end, the love you take is equal to the love you make." There is no truer statement with regard to the way entertainment works. Get out there and do what you do, mean it, and become great at it. Every ounce of yourself you give to an audience member will come back to you ten-fold.

What are your chances of success? Most bands that get major label record deals sell less than 5,000 copies. Major record labels can't make you successful. And in this DIY world of you getting your music and story out there, how do you get seen and rise above the rest? Today, success is largely built through live shows and live performances. YouTube has "made" a lot of artists. Did you ever hear of OK Go before their video "A Million Ways?" It became the most downloaded video in history in 2006 with 9 million downloads. It was a video of them performing in their backyard. And it was genius. Their next video "Here It Goes Again" featured an elaborate treadmill choreography with all the band members. Are they great guitar players? Who cares? They're great performers. That video has been downloaded over 50 million times, and that exposure has allowed them to license songs to everyone, get their records funded by huge corporations, and sell tickets all over the world. You need great songs and a certain amount of proficiency, but your live performance of those songs can bring you over the top. That is what sells you to an audience and gets them to buy your music and buy concert tickets. You may be the most talented artist in the world, but it is not a "given" that your talents will translate on stage. The combination of being a good composer and/or recording artist and stand-out stage performer is reserved for a very small number of people on earth. The ultimate goal of this book is to place you among this elite group.

A Quick Story

Many years ago I got backstage passes to see a friend play drums in a very large and prestigious concert hall along with his newly formed rock band. For the most part, the members of this band were seasoned veterans who had experienced a significant level of commercial success with other bands. This band was intended to be a sort of a "dream team" of musicians. It was the "best of the best." I remember as if it were yesterday. I hung out in the dressing room before the show. I watched them get psyched up. I also remember the show itself. They played their hearts out.

At the end of the show, they received a *"courteous"* round of applause. There was no call for an encore. It was clear to me that the audience enjoyed the performance; however, there was certainly no outpouring of affection like these band members had routinely experienced in the past.

After the show, the band was despondent. Their interpretation of receiving only "courtesy" applause was that the audience was terrible. It was the audience's fault, and the band had no desire to ever return. I knew the band's interpretation was wrong. The audience WAS good and they WERE satisfied with the performance. I had to ask myself, "What's wrong with this picture?"

After re-thinking this scenario many times, I concluded that the audience was a good audience, and they enjoyed the show, but the band had no presence or showmanship on stage. The various members of the band had always been sidemen supporting a more charismatic leader. There was no experienced front person in the band who knew how to "work the crowd." Not a single band member knew how important it was to create a relationship with the audience and take them on a journey. In their more successful endeavors, they had always accepted roles **supporting** a charismatic leader, and they never developed that talent in themselves. It was enough in those situations to just be a great musician and bandmember. This was the missing element. There was nobody present who was sensitive to the needs of the audience and who knew how to take them from one level of enjoyment to the next. There was no stage presence or charisma that the audience could bond with. My friend's band simply provided an unyielding wall of sound for 90 minutes.

Note: After this band's second compulsory album for their record label, they broke up. Today my friend is a security guard for a parking lot. (No kidding!)

The scenario described above happens too many times, around the world, every day. It happens for musicians, comedians, magicians, public speakers, and others who have the opportunity to perform for an audience, but may not know that there are tried and true methods to being a successful performer. As a musician, it's so easy to become so consumed with the technical execution of a part or a song that you are not sensitive to the needs of the audience or to the fact that there should be a very real relationship formed between the performer and the audience. Or, you may not know that an audience wants to be a part of what you're doing, and they'll respond 100 times more to you if you let them into your world.

In this book, you will be able to think about the role that the audience can play and what makes for a vibrant and memorable show. You will be able to understand why people flock to see marginally capable musicians while some of the most talented musicians on earth are sometimes ignored. You will also learn how to apply these concepts to your own performance, whether it occurs in front of friends, in a theater, a club, the boardroom of your company, or at Madison Square Garden.

As I was growing up and graduated from garage bands and practice rooms to clubs to more significant collaborations, I would constantly hear people counsel me, and my band mates, to demonstrate good **stage presence.** After hearing this wise counsel, we would emphatically agree that it is important and that we must do it. The problem was… we didn't know what stage presence meant! Although we had attended many concerts and shows watching some of the best entertainers in the world, we had absolutely no understanding of what was keeping us glued to everything that was happening on stage. This book is being written after many years of trial and error on stage combined with the analysis of the art of entertainment. It's purpose is to outline and explain these concepts in enough detail that you will be able to understand and exercise them in order to bring the quality of your stage performance up to a much higher level.

While reading this book, there may be times when you agree and other times when you disagree with certain concepts. You may even be emphatic about your disagreement. The purpose of this book is not to present things as being right or wrong, black or white. Rather, this book is intended to take a careful look at the most important aspects of stage performance. Not every theory and/or concept in this book may apply to you, but it's important to understand that they can all provide a context for analysis, self-evaluation and improvement. That is why I believe it's so important to distill these performance concepts into written form. It's my hope that performers and the industry of stage performance as a whole will benefit from committing these concepts into written form. Learn the principles described in this book, and tailor them to who you are and what you do. Make them yours!

A quick disclaimer: This book will not teach you how to sing, act, dance, play an instrument, tell jokes, or anything of the sort. The assumption is that you have mastered your craft.

The material presented in this book assumes you're "hot!" Once you're "hot," people will most likely be willing to pay to see you in action. When your extraordinary musical abilities are combined with your knowledge of the most effective way to perform in front of an audience, you may become a super-star. Let's hope you do!

Finally, this book tends to refer to musicians (vocalists and instrumentalists) more than comedians, magicians, dancers, or other performers. If you are not a musician, you may need to spend some time thinking about how these concepts may relate to your own performance. Most of the concepts included are universal, and will easily transfer to other types of presentations.

CHAPTER ONE

BASIC ENTERTAINMENT THEORY

THERE IS A THEORY OF ENTERTAINMENT JUST LIKE THERE IS A THEORY OF MUSIC. ENTERTAINMENT CONCEPTS CAN BE TAUGHT, PRACTICED, LEARNED AND APPLIED. THE APPLICATION OF THIS THEORY CAN CAUSE AN ARTIST TO BE MORE EFFECTIVE AND MEMO-RABLE FROM THE AUDIENCE'S PERSPECTIVE AND, ULTIMATELY, MORE SUCCESSFUL.

The intent of this chapter is to provide an overview of the most basic theory of stage performance and to create goals as a performer for each performance. The later chapters will drill down more deeply into the specific reasons why certain things work the way they do, and how to make them work for you.

Before a discussion regarding the basic theory of entertainment can take place, it is important to make a distinction between a technician and a performer. By this I mean a great technician (vocalist or instrumentalist) may not be a great performer. And by the same token, a great performer may not be a great technician. These are mutually exclusive abilities. Although some superstars tend to be great at both, it is more common to find artists who are technically proficient, but lost when it comes to the do's and don'ts of stage performance. It's unfortunate that the careers of these extremely talented individuals tend to be limited. Therefore, the purpose of this book is to provide the material and inspiration needed for technically proficient artists to gain the knowledge they need to be more successful on stage, and thereby give them an edge in this incredibly competitive business.

At a performance, two different entities are present for different reasons.

THE ARTIST

The artist is present to:
- Showcase his/her talent
- Entertain and please the audience
- Make as many friends in the audience as possible
- Be the cornerstone of a highly successful event

Ultimately, the degree of success during the show depends not only upon the amount of talent the artist possesses and exhibits, but also upon the quality of a relationship that the artist develops with the audience. If a show fails, the artist has no one else to blame, but himself.

The amount of success achieved is directly proportional to the degree of talent and the degree of entertainment skills possessed and exercised by the artist. These performance skills involve the actions of giving of themselves and their talent for the benefit of the audience and ultimately for the success of the show. The audience reciprocates by giving back their attention and applause.

THE AUDIENCE

The audience is present not only to be entertained by, but also to celebrate their affection for the particular artist who is on the bill. Their hope is to be mesmerized and entertained as a result of the interaction between themselves and the artist.

It is the responsibility of the artist to initiate and maintain this interaction.

"For every action there is an equal and opposite reaction."
—Sir Isaac Newton

THE GOLDEN RULE

There is a variation of the golden rule that says, "He who has the gold… rules." This applies to an audience. Since it is the audience who pays for the tickets, CDs, DVDs, t-shirts, and other assorted memorabilia; they are the ones with the gold. Therefore, a fitting part of any concert performance should be an opportunity to pay tribute to the audience. With this in mind, the performer should be constantly concerned about the state of the audience, precisely because they are the ones who "rule."

The best way to pay tribute to an audience is to establish a mutually rewarding relationship from the start of the performance, and increase the rewards as the show progresses. By the end of the performance, there should be bonds of mutual caring, concern, and affection that result in the audience jumping out of their seats to demand an encore. When this happens, it is obvious that the performers have done their jobs.

There are many ways to establish a rewarding relationship with an audience. To begin, it's important to note that a paying audience is typically ready, willing, and able to be actively involved in the show. They want to clap for you. They want to scream for you. Otherwise, they would never have come to your show at all! It is very important that the audience be allowed and even encouraged to express themselves. Just as a baby is surprised and delighted when he/she eventually learns how to manipulate his/her parents, the members of an audience are equally surprised and delighted when they learn how they can affect or alter the course of the show. It is, therefore, of crucial importance that the performers work to involve the audience throughout the show in order to create a magical and memorable event.

This is not rocket science. It all boils down to the basic concepts of:

GIVE AND YOU WILL RECEIVE

KARMA

THE GOLDEN RULE

CHAPTER TWO

BEFORE YOU WALK
ON STAGE

Individuals exhibit performance style in many different ways. Obviously, it should be stated that performing a rock concert is very different than making a presentation in front of 10 executives at a weekly board meeting. The elements for success in either, though, are the same. You have to go in knowing a few basic concepts, and then you must be prepared to carry out your performance based on this knowledge.

Performance is not a one-sided affair. Performance is a relationship between yourself and your audience. Each has a very distinct role, but it is the depth of the relationship you form with the audience that can make you or break you.

Do a little soul searching before you walk on stage. It'll make you a more confident person, and therefore a more confident performer. In any relationship, you should know yourself and be the best you can be before you are ready for a relationship with someone else, namely, the audience.

KNOW WHO YOU ARE AND WHAT YOU ARE
TRYING TO CONVEY

In any relationship, it helps to know yourself first before you try to build a relationship with someone else. The thing you have to consider when performing for any audience is: What are you trying to convey? Are you on stage to "rock the house" and give people the most incredible rock show they've ever seen? Or, are you on stage to give the audience an intimate portrait of a collection of songs that are incredibly personal and heartfelt? Are you electric or acoustic? Defining your goal in detail is imperative to your success at achieving your goal.

Here are a few questions to answer honestly and in detail before you step near a stage:

1. What do I have to offer? In other words, why would someone come see me instead of someone else?
2. Why do I do what I do? What is my motivation?
3. What makes me different than other performers? Why am I special?
4. What am I trying to convey with my performance?

People come to a show to be moved in some way. They want to personally get something out of the experience . . .to be inspired, to feel connected, to feel some passion. Rocking the house or playing heartfelt songs are your "delivery devices" for moving an audience. Know who you are as a performer in order to move your audience effectively.

KNOW YOUR STRENGTHS

Every person and/or performer has strengths. Drawing on these strengths when organizing a show is of paramount importance. You can and will develop additional performance strengths as time goes on, but always be true to yourself. It is said that people can always sniff out a fraud. People know when you're not being true to who you are. For example, if Britney Spears were not attractive and a great dancer, it would have been pointless to build her career on huge pop productions carried out live through elaborate choreography and sexy lyrics. Build your stage persona based on your core knowledge of yourself. Take time to examine who you are and what you stand for. Do some true soul searching and define who you are as a person and performer.

A few questions you should answer:

1. What are my strengths as an artist and/or performer?
2. What are my strengths as a person that could help me on stage?
3. What do I do better than anyone else?
4. What values and/or personal beliefs do I have that define who I am?
5. What settings am I comfortable in? Do I work well with others or am I better "solo"?

This concept of "knowing your strengths" applies to much more than stage performance. It can apply to the very core of who you are as an artist. For example, write or choose songs that reflect who you are and what your personal belief system is. That way, they will come across on stage as being authentic.

Do you think Muse's Matt Bellamy believes what he's singing in "Uprising"? I do. Do you believe Aretha Franklin when she's asking for your "Respect"? I do. These two artists know their strengths and they choose and/or write their material to enhance and showcase those strengths. And their live performance always brings those strengths to a new level. Muse's stage set-ups and lighting rivals any band in the world. And he has armies of people that come for the entire experience of the show he puts on. And it's him through and through...every note and every moment of it. Every audience member can feel that. **Never underestimate the intuition of an audience**. They know if you're posing as something you're not. They can sniff it out! Focus on your strengths and your passions. Are you a great vocalist? Feature that. Are you funny? Find ways to incorporate humor. Do you have something to say about politics? Say it. Are you angry? Write it into a song and let it out on stage every night. Feature your strengths. Walk on stage knowing what is going to set you apart from anyone else. Let that knowledge and certainty of self develop into a confidence and energy that will draw people in. Give people something real, and they will respond with a similarly real and respective reply.

KNOW YOUR AUDIENCE

It is imperative that you know who your audience is comprised of. Who comes or would come to see you? Who do you appeal to as a general rule? Are your audience members high schoolers or baby boomers? Are they primarily well educated, or less educated? What do they eat for breakfast? What do they like to do in their spare time?

A perfect example of knowing your audience is Larry the Cable Guy. He's a southern redneck comedian, and that's his audience. His jokes all deal with "white trash" southern humor. He makes no apologies for his southern twang and/or trailer trash infused jokes. He knows himself, and what's funny to him. He lives it on stage. He's not trying to reach out to the upper class or the urban audience. He knows his audience, and he caters to them, incredibly successfully, I might add!

In advertising and marketing, it is imperative to "know your demographic." How does this apply to you as a performer? It not only lets you choose where you play so that your demographic can attend, but it allows you to build a show based on what your audience will be attracted to and will enjoy. If you've never considered who buys your CDs or who comes to your shows, take a closer look. Invariably some similarities will present themselves. You can use this knowledge to better gauge what your audience will react to and how you should communicate with them.

Another perfect example of someone knowing his demographic is the classic jazz saxophonist, Cannonball Adderley. If you delve into his old recordings or ask people who knew him, they'll say that he was an articulate and personable performer and artist. He had a special knack for relating to his audience, the jazz audience. Let's examine the demographic of his audience. Progressive Jazz was a newer art form at the time he was performing. His particular audience was comprised of hipster city dwellers that prided themselves on being in on the coolness of the trend of jazz. They were educated. They were interested not only in the music, but the scene itself. It was a lifestyle. The real jazz audience at that time even delved into the talents of the particular players on stage and the performers on the records. They didn't only come to see the front person or bandleader. Cannonball Adderley drew from all of this knowledge. He even opened his "Live in New York" album with an ode to his audience. He said …

> *"We've made a lot of records in nightclubs, especially in California at the famous Lighthouse in Hermosa Beach and at the Jazz Workshop in San Francisco and the reason we selected those rooms was because the audiences were so hip that we could, you know, just play what we wanted to play without being bothered and everybody dug it, you see.*

We've never made a live album in New York because, for some reason, we have never really felt the kind of thing that we've wanted to feel from the audience, which has nothing to do with acceptance, applause or appreciation. It's the atmosphere. You know - you get a lot of people who are supposed to be hip, you know, and they act like they're supposed to be hip, which makes a big difference, you see what I mean?

Now we have especially been impressed with the audience here at the matinee performance at the Village Vanguard. We think that this is the kind of audience that is the real jazz audience. And we want to thank you for making it possible – for being so really hip. You know hipness is not a state of mind – it's a fact of life, you see what I mean? You don't decide you're hip. It just happens that way. You see what I mean?

So, today we're doing our first New York live album courtesy of you, the audience. Thank you very much."

Julian "Cannonball" Adderley
Village Vanguard, NYC, 1962
The Cannonball Adderley Sextet in New York
Riverside RLP 404

Who couldn't appreciate that as an audience? Before one note has been played, the person you came to admire and be entertained by has complimented you personally. In between songs, Cannonball would draw further from his knowledge that his audience was interested in more than just hearing him play. They were educated, cutting edge people, and they thrived on knowledge. He gave it to them. He'd introduce every song with a story of why it was written, who wrote it, and maybe give a witty insight or two into the actual writing of it. He featured his musicians both musically and in word on stage. He gave the audience everything he knew they wanted. Cannonball Adderley's success was based not only on his incredible musicianship and writing skills, but also on his ability to form a strong bond with his audience.

COMMITMENT

One aspect of performance that is constantly overlooked is the commitment level to your show. Whatever genre is portrayed, whether heavy metal or a swinging jazz trio, you have to commit 100% to it. Live it. Breathe it. You can never "break character." People need to walk away knowing exactly who you are and what you do. The audience needs to believe that who they see up there is who you really are. That's why it's easier to know yourself first and tailor your performance to exactly who you are than to pose as something that isn't really you!

For example, Saturday Night Live did a skit a few years ago based on this very concept. They had a handful of rappers on as guests of a popular talk show. During the interviews on the talk show, the rappers were in character, and talking about the street and where they came from, the hood, etc. When the commercial break came, they all became different people. One was on the phone with his stockbroker discussing when to buy high or low, with no remnant of the "street" accent or slang. Another was speaking in an almost British accent about selling his real estate. The point was, that the public doubted whether some of these gangster rappers really lived what they rapped. They played the part for the people on TV, but when the cameras were off, you realized the façade they showed you on stage really didn't reflect who they were in real life. So…leave it to Saturday Night Live to expose this notion and poke fun at them!

The point is, your audience needs to feel that you are 100% invested in what you are doing and what you are singing or playing about. They need to know that the "you" they know is the real you. If <u>you're</u> not convinced, <u>they</u> won't be either! Commit yourself fully.

THE ONLY THING TO FEAR IS FEAR ITSELF

Everyone's been on a first date. Most people would agree that first dates are uncomfortable. Both parties are getting to know each other for the first time. Neither is comfortable with the other, and both want to impress. Being on stage is a bit like a first date. Chances are that some of your audience have never seen you or have never been in the same room with you. They may know something about you after listening to your music on CDs, radio, or the internet. But this is your first chance to make a personal connection.

With a first date, awkwardness on both sides is understood and might even be entertaining or endearing. However, as a performer, fear is a killer. You are forming a relationship with the audience, but you are not allowed to show your fear. You are the one that must be in control.

The concept that dogs can innately sense fear is a widely accepted notion. Audiences are no different. If you doubt yourself at any turn, they will sense it. You have to commit fully to what you're doing and carry it through with the utmost confidence and belief.

You may ask, "How do I deal with my fear and not let the audience know?" If you are not the artist or performer who is innately comfortable on stage (and believe me, many struggle arduously with this one!) there are a few options.

1. Fake it.

A wise man once said, **"The only thing to fear is fear itself."** Wise words, but fear is hard to shake. Until you're completely comfortable sharing yourself on stage and not worrying about it, just pretend like you believe in yourself and/or what you're portraying. Are you scared that people won't like you? Pretend that you're confident. Are you scared that you're not the best vocalist in the world? Pretend that you're the best singer on the planet. Drill that into your mind and live that reality, not the one that's paralyzing you. Sometimes that goes a long way towards fighting off the fear that an audience can incite. You might even fool *yourself* after a while and loosen up and not have to fake it any more. That's the idea. Fake it until you make it, or at least until you make yourself believe that you're in your rightful place on stage and you're comfortable. People want to like you. They want to believe you. They want to be entertained. That's why they're out sitting in a seat watching you. Be the star you perceive yourself to be, even if you feel foolish at times or you doubt yourself. Fake it until you can get past your fear and/or lack of confidence.

2. Find a "happy place."

If panic sets in and you freeze up, find a place in your head that takes you away from the panic that has set in. Pretend you're there. Pretend that you're doing your show there, in your comfort zone.

In Adam Sandler's movie "Happy Gilmore," his character was asked to go to his "happy place" to help him succeed as a golfer. He went to his "happy place" which consisted of his female co-star scantily clad in a bustier carrying two pitchers of beer, his grandmother winning big money at the slot machines, and a little person riding a tricycle around the golf course in a cowboy outfit. This may not be your idea of a good time, but it was his and it got him through some hard times in the movie. Find your very own happy place, whether it's on a beach or riding a roller coaster at Disneyworld.

3. Picture the audience in their underwear!
This is an oldie but a goodie. And it may seem trivial or stupid, but sometimes the audience can become scary. Hundreds, or maybe thousands of eyes are watching you intently, and you are on the spot in every way in front of them. Take their power away. Picture them in their underwear, much less ominous or threatening now than when they were with all their clothes on. It may even make you smile, which will signal to the audience that everything is all right!!

4. Pretend you're playing to your closest friends.
Put the faces of your friends and/or family on the audience member's heads. This will make you feel like you're in front of a friendly crowd, not one that you're sure is going to judge you or boo you off the stage. Close your eyes for a second and pretend that your best friend is sitting across from you listening. Place the faces of your friends on the faces of different people scattered around the crowd. Maybe Aunt Bea is in the balcony and your neighbor George is to your right hand side in the third row. It helps to think that the audience is on your side and friendly! And it will allow you to relax and perform to your best ability.

5. Focus before you walk on stage.
A lot can happen backstage. It can be a cacophony of events, from meet and greets to photos with fans to going over new parts with your band to getting dressed and warmed up. Take a few

moments for yourself before you hit the stage for your show. Know what you're going to do. Focus on it and live it for a few moments in your mind. Think about what you're about to perform. Be "in the moment" and in control of your show. That focus will help you deal with any fear that may come your way.

6. Tell yourself what you need to hear.
There are voices in all of our heads sometimes that tell us we're not good enough or that we're in over our heads. Some of the most successful performers I've met have confided in me that they have huge, sometimes crippling feelings of self-doubt before every performance. My own grandmother was a rare and gifted coloratura soprano. But she was terrified to step on stage, and so she didn't. What a shame that her stage fright stopped her from sharing a true gift with others.

These voices seem very real, and it's easy to get caught up in feelings of inadequacy. Don't get caught up. Drown the negative voices out and tell yourself that you are good enough. Tell yourself you have a gift to share that is beautiful. Tell yourself that this is your show, your music, and your evening. Let your personal energy embrace that power. It's yours. Sometimes you just have to remind yourself of that. It's bigger than the negativity that rears it's ugly head sometimes. Tell yourself that this is your night, and you're the one who should be on stage. Remind yourself that you have something important to share with the audience. After that, get out of your head. Move into the present and remind yourself to connect with the audience. Focus your newly found power on them, and embrace the new relationship you're going to have with them. Walk out there full of confidence instead of getting caught up in your head.

7. Take charge.
It can be very intimidating to walk into a room of people that you don't know and make them feel at ease when in reality

you're scared to death. One of my first road shows as a solo artist I opened up for Al Jarreau, and I was scheduled to do a "meet and greet" with him before the show with some contest winners. I arrived early to a room full of fans that were excited but very hesitant to come up and approach me. I stood on the side of the room and didn't make eye contact with anyone. I didn't know what to do! Al Jarreau walked in and immediately waved to everyone in the room and said "Welcome, I'm so glad you're here." He motioned for one man to come get his CD signed. He just walked in the middle of the room and took over. It was a huge lesson to me at the time. He walked through the door and made everyone feel at ease and feel like he was their friend, while I was standing uncomfortably in the corner being shy. He took charge and created the atmosphere in the room, rather than letting his fear or the fear of the fans dictate the atmosphere. Take charge and create the feel of any room you're in, whether you're on stage or off. You're the star. It's your job to make everyone feel comfortable and at ease.

MYSTIQUE: CREATING THE "IT" FACTOR

Mystique: *A fascinating aura of mystery, awe and power surrounding someone or something.*

If you have ever watched a full season of the hit reality TV series "American Idol," you have watched a select group of performers from across the nation undergo a gradual transformation from typical people you might meet on the street to well-groomed and dressed, articulate, savvy, more confident and capable professional entertainment types. The transition between how they appeared during their initial auditions across the country and the manner in which they presented themselves during the final weeks of the competition is radical and dynamic. This is no accident. First, they have the benefit of industry professionals who coached them throughout the process. The sharper ones kept their eyes, ears and minds open and, in the process of doing so, learned a lot. Plus, the reality of being around such a talented group of highly motivated artists who are struggling hard to strengthen their game has the effect of rubbing off on all of them. They carry and express themselves much better than when they first auditioned. Are they better singers a few weeks in? Sometimes. But the overwhelming change to me is their confidence and newly found power. They have an aura about them. They are slowly but surely gaining that "it" factor that combines talent with the look and the feel of success. Is it a fluke or an intangible "something" that just some people have? It is no fluke.

A person who has not only had the benefit of high-level professional experience but has also experienced a lot of interesting things will typically stand out from a crowd. It is not cockiness, but rather a confidence of experience.

You're building your arsenal of weapons to gain your own "it" factor. You're already excellent at what you do, you know who you are and what you stand for, and you live that reality every day. You tame your fears. And now you must refine the details of what makes you special. Combine these weapons, and you will win any war.

Have you ever been in a room full of people when a superstar walked in the room? Usually they stop traffic. I know I stopped in my tracks the first time I walked by David Bowie. Literally, three people walking behind me bumped into me as I stopped and stared. He had that mystique, that "it" factor. He was so stylized and walked with an air of confidence. He lit up the room and carried himself with an almost regal quality.

Can you learn to exude mystique and build your own "it" factor? Absolutely. It'll take some soul searching. It'll take some real world experience and the confidence that comes from the life you're making happen for yourself. There are a few common sense things to think about when building your personal mystique and "it" factor.

The First 10 Seconds are the Most Important

As soon as the audience catches their first glimpse of you, they begin checking you out from head to toe. They evaluate your clothes, your hair, your shoes, how you stand, how you move, whether you seem to be happy to be there or not, if you're overweight or thin, or whether you are more interested in yourself than anything else. Are you having fun? Do you seem up to the task of creating a memorable event that will include them? Do you look like a winner? Do they like you? Do they think you're cool?

Audiences and fans usually want their idols and stars to be "set apart" from the rest. Some perfect examples are Gwen Stefani, Bruno Mars, Madonna, Jennifer Lopez, Jimi Hendrix, Lady Gaga, and Prince. Each one of these artists has set him or herself apart from the crowd. Each has sold millions of records. And you could get a detailed description with regard to what makes them different from the rest by asking almost anyone in the world. Being "set apart" means you do things a bit differently from everyone else. You have your own personal style. You stand out from the crowd. For example, Bjork has always stood apart from anyone else. She has a very unique personal sense of style and identity. I've never even seen anyone try to copy her successfully. She wears space suits and swan dresses and even fancies herself from a different planet in some interviews. She is an individualist with her music and her image. She's made herself unmistakable as an artist, and therefore has built a career on that mystique and her own "it" factor.

In the early '90s, Kurt Cobain introduced anti-fashion. This was his way of being "set apart." Instead of dressing like other musicians of his day, mostly dolled up hair bands, he wore plaid flannel shirts as his personal statement of rebellion to the industry and his fans. Kurt Cobain was so successful introducing his revolt of style that it became fashionable immediately.

Lady Gaga has built her career on changing her image constantly and always staying ahead of the trend. She creates trends, rather than follows them. She does the unexpected. She goes for shock value, and has created super-stardom from it.

There should be something about you that stands out. Would you idolize someone who looked like your next-door neighbor? Not likely. I usually idolize people that have the guts to do or wear something that maybe I don't have the guts to do or wear. This doesn't mean you have to be freaky. Take **your** style and taste, though, to the extreme and stand out.

Create Your Look

1. Hair
Hairstyles come in many shapes and colors and can hugely affect the way you're viewed by people. The girls in the B52s have huge bouffant hairdos. It gives them a fun, quirky image that really sets them apart. Snoop Dogg always has crazy braids standing out and/or in ponytails. Pink defined herself with a pink head of hair as a new artist. Lenny Kravitz waved his dreads around on stage like a rock star.

There are many resources available for you to come up with your look. Check out monthly hairstyle magazines. Talk to your hairstylist and ask what he or she would recommend to you based on your face shape and/or personal style. Try on wigs and/or hairpieces to get an idea of what different styles might look like on you. There are even websites that you can upload a photo of yourself and try on different hairstyles so you can see yourself differently.

Take time and choose a hairstyle that works for you and the image that you're portraying.

2. Makeup
(This is not just for girls…think KISS or Duran Duran or even Marilyn Manson)
Makeup can make a huge difference in portraying an image on stage. Actresses like Marilyn Monroe chose classic glamorous makeup to portray her iconic sexy image. Ozzy Osbourne chose black eyeliner to create the image of the "Prince of Darkness," while Marilyn Manson chose contact lenses in different colors and opacities and white makeup with odd colored eyeshadows, etc. to create a mesmerizing androgeny. Many female artists of the 70s chose no makeup and/or no bras to make their statement. They were "natural," earthy and unaffected and that's what they wanted to portray to their audiences. The members of KISS built their identities from their personal makeup. Paul Stanley had the star on his eye. Peter Criss had the cat face with whiskers, Ace Frehley was "the Spaceman," and Gene Simmons had blood dripping from his freakishly long tongue. Take into consideration the fact that these guys wore this makeup for every show, public appearance, band outing, press opportunity, etc. for years. They never broke character from their makeup.

Take time to develop your "look." Draw upon who you are and what you want to convey as an artist. And know that what you decide on is who you are going to have to be for a long time. Just as you need to be careful to write songs you want to play for the next 30+ years, you need to find a look that you can believe in and portray for the next 30+ years. Try different things if you're unsure of what's you. Find people you relate to and take different beauty tips from each one. Try it on yourself and try to make it yours. You don't want to look exactly like another artist, but it doesn't hurt to steal a few ideas here and there! Just as musically you learn by imitation and slowly create your own style, so you can learn stylistically by imitating your icons and making it your own after some experimentation.

Professional help is always a great tool. There are so many resources out there to draw from to create your look. You can go into makeup counters in almost any department store and get a makeover. Tell the makeup artist what you are looking for and what style is you. Have some fun! Learn from what you like and don't like in your makeovers. MAC is a more stage oriented makeup company, and has stores across the country. Their makeup artists will help you design a look that's right for you. They're known for more cutting edge colors and makeup applications. Or, spend time experimenting on yourself at home until you get the look you want. It's worth the time and effort.

Focus on your personal style and what you're trying to convey as an artist. Let makeup work for you to express that.

3. Fashion: Clothes and shoes
Fashion sense is a defining part of any performer's look. Just as makeup and hairstyles change people's perception of you, fashion completes the process.

Here are a few thoughts on defining your own fashion sense. First of all, make it your own. Prince didn't buy off the rack. He had his clothes made. Michael Jackson wore a glove on only one hand. Beyonce used her mother's sewing and design prowess to give "Destiny's Child" and Beyonce as a solo artist a "look" that was different than anyone else's look. Carrie Bradshaw (Sarah Jessica Parker) from "Sex and the City" was known for her Manolo Blahnik and Jimmy Choo shoes. Gwen Stefani charted out designs on paper and had a local seamstress create them for her. She later started her own clothing line, "L.A.M.B."

The point being, find your own sense of style. Exploit it. There is a reason people dress like their favorite artists. Their favorite artists are trendsetters. They dress themselves in unique and interesting ways. They shop at stores that carry items not found everywhere else. They don't casually select and wear clothing. Everything must fit perfectly and go together to create a special effect. They live their look and image. This is what you need to do. Take time and effort to put together outfits. Be a trendsetter, not a trend follower. The right "look" will immediately tell your audience who you are. That's priceless.

All of this does not require huge amounts of money. Madonna created her look when she lived in NYC and had no money. She found clothes out of dumpsters and thrift stores and made them into a "look." You don't need money to create a look and an image. You just need imagination and you need to know yourself. Look carefully and buy intelligently.

There are many resources at your disposal for creating your look. Many celebrities use personal stylists or personal shoppers to go after a certain look for them. It's always a good move if you can afford it, to involve experts. You could hire a stylist to put together a collection of stage clothes and every day clothes that portray your image. Sometimes an expert or professional will be able to help you bring out the best in yourself, even if you're not sure what that is! Find people who are knowledgeable, trustworthy and truthful with you. Yes, this will cost some money, but they will take the project seriously and give you excellent advice. Again, don't try to be something you're not. Be who you are…just better.

There are also many fashion magazines that focus on the latest trends and collections. Read, look, and stay current and take ideas from different people. Stealing ideas isn't a crime! A wise man once said that, "Originality is the art of masking your influences." That applies to everything, not just fashion!

After you've soul searched and put together your "look," here are few pointers as to how to wear your new look:

1. Exhibit your fashion sense all the time, not just on stage. If you saw P Diddy at the local Starbucks in plaid golf pants and a button down shirt, that would go against everything you've ever seen from him as an artist. Not good. You don't have to be perfect all the time, but at least stay true to your identity and sense of style no matter if you're walking your dog or on stage performing.
2. Develop your sense of self-awareness and confidence. Walk tall. Have a sense of purpose and self esteem. Nothing completes a look like confidence.
3. Wear clothing on stage that fits what you're doing. If you sweat a lot, plan for short sleeves and fabrics that breathe. Are you playing a festival in the sun or a theater in air conditioning with a great light show? I'd choose the outfit that sparkles for a show with lights, not one where

they will get lost in the sunshine. Do you play an instrument that can get tangled up in fringe from a jacket or shirt? Lose the fringe. Do you need a place to clip a wireless in-ear monitor pack? Think that out when choosing your outfit. Do you always perform in your bare feet? Think twice when the stage is old and splintering. Know your situations before putting together your stage attire.

A fan or audience member wants to feel like the object of their attention (the artist) is worthy. Otherwise, they could just be another person walking down the street. Dennis Miller of "Saturday Night Live" once said, "A true rock star will always light up a room." So, light up the room. If you walk into a shopping mall on tour somewhere in small town America, you should be prepared to be stared at. You should stand out and make a statement wherever you are, whatever you are doing. Make that a quest.

Take time with your image. Get good advice. Make yourself the best you can be. Don't be fooled by people who are going to sell you out or give you bad advice. You may remember the children's story, "The Emperor's New Clothes." The emperor was fooled into believing he was wearing the most exclusive clothing ever created. In fact, he was naked and there was nobody present who would confront him. In the end, the emperor looked foolish. Know yourself and don't be taken in by the latest trend. You are your own person creating your own trends. When you have decided on an image that works for you, you should feel an air of added confidence and strength. Once you have your image, you're ready to walk on stage!

CHAPTER THREE

THE NASCAR EFFECT: HOW TO MEET AND LEAD THE AUDIENCE

"Drafting"

As you know from the chapters above, it is very important to know who you are, know what you're trying to convey as an artist, and have your own mystique, or look, to set you apart as a performer. Next, you must capture the attention of the audience, establish a relationship with them, and lead them through a meaningful and mutually rewarding experience from the beginning of the show to the end.

If you lead effectively, your audience will be able to follow closely and feed off of your power and artistry. If you lead poorly, you could lose your connection, and be alone on stage without the support of your audience. Never run off and leave your audience.

TAKING THE STAGE

The first 10 seconds are the most crucial to winning over an audience.

How you walk onto the stage is important. It gives the audience an idea of who and what is important. If you walk onto the stage initially looking at the other band members and their equipment, it appears that (1) you think you are more important than the audience or (2) you are ignoring the audience. If you walk onto the stage immediately looking out into the audience to see everyone, you convey the impression that you can't wait to become friends with everyone. This immediately gives the audience a feeling of importance, and ultimately causes them to like you from the very beginning.

The best way to prepare for walking onto the stage is to have all of your equipment, microphones, guitars, drumsticks, etc. ready so that you can pick them up and/or put them on without even thinking about it. This enables you to be free to check out the audience from the first step you take on stage, and this starts the show off in the most personal and effective way possible. You're confident, ready to give as a performer, and this is your time. Look them straight in the eyes, and then rock them!

NOTHING SUCCEEDS LIKE SUCCESS

Walk on stage as if you own it and you belong there. Exude confidence and success. Don't confuse the terms confidence and success with cockiness. Cocky people are generally not well liked. On the other hand, people don't want to follow someone who appears to be unsure of themselves or worse, a loser. They will follow a winner anywhere. **A great smile will do wonders.** It imparts the feeling that, "I know what I'm doing. I've done it a million times before. Come along with me. This is going to be great!"

BE YOU

One of the difficulties in explaining the best way to meet the audience is that performance styles can be so wildly different. For example, the well-known, high energy rock group "KISS" comes out blasting and uses a lot of intricate lighting and pyrotechnics. On the other end of the spectrum, jazz singer Norah Jones comes out performing a more low-key, sensitive marriage of music and lyrics. These two approaches are completely different, but they are completely correct for each act. The higher-power rock group needs to establish themselves as such. The warm and smooth singer-songwriter needs to likewise establish the environment and level of intimacy that facilitates the best possible presentation of his or her material. The important thing to consider is how you and your group intend to meet the audience. Do your best to make a statement regarding who you are. Establish your character very early, and you will be able to take the audience on a journey from there.

Many years ago a very famous R&B singer-songwriter, who had a number one hit song on the Billboard Charts, was performing a live concert. After the house lights were dimmed and the singer took the stage, the audience went wild. They were anxious to hear some of the most brilliantly executed R&B music of the day. Instead of playing R&B, this artist started playing old standard songs, as if he were the piano player in a nightclub lounge. The crowd was forgiving, however, they were a bit disappointed. The expectation that a certain character would emerge from the stage at the outset didn't happen. Once again, establish your true character early so you can move to take the crowd on a journey. Don't start off on a tangent. You can journey toward this, but a tangent should never start or end a show.

After you have played your opening musical segment, the audience will applaud. Respond to the audience's applause by thanking them and by making a statement that will help to establish the tone of the show for the night.

YOU CONTROL THE SHOW

Control of the show is a simple concept that can either make you or break you. Part of any successful relationship is knowing who's in charge. **You are in charge.** There are no exceptions to this hard and fast rule. You should be in control of a number of things, including the overall feel of the show, the content, the amount and quality of interaction with the audience, and even the pacing of the show. You should always go in with these things in mind. Even though it is the audience who is buying the tickets, you should realize that they are paying **you** to be in charge.

Actors are always taught to never break character and to never allow hecklers or interruptive elements of any type to break their concentration and performance. As musical performers, some-how that's never taught to us! But the concept works for any type of performer. Is there someone in the audience that is yelling out a request for a song continually? Is it distracting people from what you're doing on stage? Is it distracting you from what you are doing? Move the show along. Are girls in the front row fainting and being carried away on stretchers because they're so excited? Let security take care of everyone while you play. Don't lose sight of what you're on stage to do.

Later in the book, I will describe in more detail different ways of handling these types of distractions or the types of fighting for control that you may experience from hecklers.

CARDINAL RULE:

Never give up control of your show to anyone or anything.

There are many things to divert you from your goal of putting on a great show. Lighting can fail, microphones can go out, a streaker can waltz by behind you, your guitarist might be having a bad day, or the woman in the front row is reaching up constantly to shake your hand as you're trying to play an instrument. Whatever it is, it is not more important than your show. Take time to address things that need to be addressed, but never lose control of the show you've worked so hard to create and carry out.

THE ROLE OF THE FRONT PERSON VERSUS SIDEPERSON

The position of the front person is the most important on stage since he/she is the primary person responsible for establishing and maintaining a personal and productive relationship with the audience. The front person is the primary communicator with the audience, and therefore takes on most of the responsibility. This is done by:

- Constantly monitoring the progress of the show
- Continually evaluating the audience response
- Saying the right things at the right time
- Making timely adjustments as necessary to maximize opportunities
- Making sure the supporting performers are properly recognized
- Making sure the most crucial parts of the show, especially the beginning and ending, are executed properly

This position is key with regard to manifesting and projecting the appropriate energy level to the audience as well as to the supporting performers. In some ways, a comparison might be made to the conductor of an orchestra or the ringmaster of a circus. Some historic examples of great front people include: Mick Jagger, Steven Tyler, Prince, Chris Martin, Beyoncé, Gwen Stefani, and Usher. The front person not only urges the audience onward, but the supporting performers as well.

Note: In the case of an ensemble where other members share part of the fronting duties (duo, trio, etc.) each member is equally responsible. All performers should learn these concepts, since every performer should be aware of communication and performance concepts and skills.

FACTOR IN YOUR INTENSITY LEVEL

When accepting applause after the first musical segment and speaking to the audience for the first time, performers must be careful to speak with a level of intensity commensurate with the current intensity of the room. For instance, after the big Foo Fighters show opener, the crowd will be going crazy. With the band performing at a high energy level and the crowd going crazy, Dave Grohl (the front person) should be energetic and enthusiastic. For Dave to come across meek and mellow, in this situation, would be a mistake. Conversely, if someone like Natalie Cole were to speak with a hyped up tone after her opening segment, she would come across as phony and weird. **You must match the intensity level of the moment with how you speak to the audience**.

Once you have firmly established your character at the beginning of the show, and have responded to the audience with the correct level of intensity, you can now help the flow of the show by re-adjusting your intensity to effectively segue through the upcoming segments. If you are transitioning into a segment that is more mellow or low-key, you may want to take your intensity level down a notch or two. Likewise, you may want to take the intensity level up a few notches if you know you will be transitioning into a segment that is more upbeat. This can be accomplished by adjusting your level of animation and the pitch or intensity of your speech. Either way, use your initial intensity level, as initially established by your music and the enthusiasm of the crowd, and make slight adjustments from there as you take the audience on their journey.

THE NASCAR EFFECT

The term NASCAR Effect refers to a racing technique known as "drafting." To be able to benefit from "drafting," a race car driver positions his race car directly behind another car. If he is able to keep his car relatively close behind another car, it will be pulled along the racetrack saving gas mileage since the engine won't have to work as hard. However, if the car in front accelerates too quickly and pulls away, the second car can lose its "draft" and end up falling behind and operating alone. In this analogy, the car in front is the performer. The car directly behind is the audience. This is also true with stage performance. The artist must carefully lead an audience and let them feed off of his/her talents and stage presence. To take "drafting" a step further, and incorporate the idea of intensity, the artist must determine the audience's level of intensity at the beginning of the show and lead them forward without leaving them behind in a cloud of dust. If the artist is not careful, he/she may find the audience is not following along. The point is that the performer should always stay connected to and slightly ahead of the intensity and emotion of the audience. There are a few dangerous scenarios to avoid:

1. Being too hyped on stage while the audience is watching calmly and unimpressed.
2. Being too low-key while the audience wants to party.
3. Feeling disconnected, therefore causing the audience to feel disconnected.
4. Portraying something the audience wasn't ready for.

There is a very famous story about Ricky Nelson playing Madison Square Garden (thank you to Sandy Friedman at Rogers and Cowan for this story!). In 1972, Ricky Nelson released the song "Garden Party," his last top 40 hit, written about his 1971 Madison Square Garden appearance where he was booed for playing his new material instead of his "hits." He had a persona and identity that he was known for. He neglected to portray that, and chose to try something completely new at this show. His audience didn't come to see that. They came to see the 50s star they knew and loved. The audience became disappointed and booed him.

Each of the previous scenarios makes for a disconnected show. Therefore, it's better to lead the audience from one transition to the next without the audience becoming lost or disenfranchised.

Figure 1 below illustrates the correct intensity level between the performer and the audience. The performer starts at a certain level. This level depends upon the characteristics of the act. Once the proper level has been established, and a connection is made, the performer can use the NASCAR Effect to lead the audience throughout the various segments of the show.

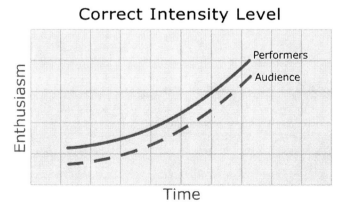

Figure 1: NASCAR Effect - Correct Intensity Level

Figure 1 above is the correct approach. The intensity level is slightly higher than that of the audience. This allows the performers to "lift" the audience up to the desired level of intensity and lead them to additional levels of enjoyment and interaction.

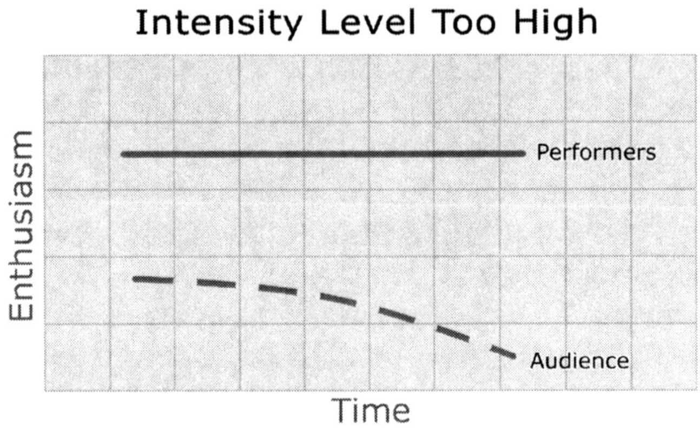

Intensity Level Too High

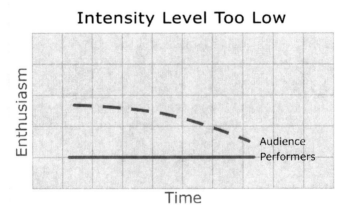

Figure 2: Intensity Level Too High

As you can see from Figure 2 above, the performers have alienated the audience by starting out too intensely. The performers remain separated from the intensity level of the audience causing them to eventually lose contact with one another.

Intensity Level Too Low

Figure 3: Intensity Level Too Low

As you can see from Figure 3 above, the performers are bringing the enthusiastic audience down since they did not correctly calculate the intensity level of the audience. A previously excited audience will re-think their decision to come to the show, and possibly to future ones.

STAY ONE STEP AHEAD OF YOUR AUDIENCE

Is there a way to know how the audience will respond before the show starts? The answer is…"Yes." To find out, you should become informed of the news, major events, feelings and attitudes of the local community and you must be perceptive. There are many more outside stimuli that affect people's moods and reactions, than just the immediate relationship between a performer and audience. Be aware of them.

Gather Intelligence

When you arrive in a new country or city, it is a great idea to make friends with anyone local. Ask a few questions:

- How is the local economy?
- Are people happy (in general)?
- How are the sports teams in the area doing?
- Has anything exciting happened recently in the area? If so, what was it?
- What problems are people experiencing?
- How do the local people feel about performers from our city, state, country, etc.?
- Have there been any disastrous events that have taken place around here lately?
- How do people feel about the show tonight?

- Have there been other performers here recently? If so, who were they?
- How were other performers received?
- Is there anything I should be aware of?

In most cases, several of the answers you receive will be surprising. Instead of hearing that everything is okay and the show should be stellar, you will find that certain things are <u>not</u> okay. For example, there could have been the death of a popular young person in the area and people have been grieving for days. Or, the last band to come through the area was a major disappointment. If your list of questions is long enough, you will learn very interesting things about the feelings and sentiments of the people who will soon be the target of your performance. If there has been a disaster of some kind, you may want to mention it in a respectful tone at an appropriate moment during the show. This will help the audience to understand that you have a personal interest in their local community. If there has been a positive event such as a local sports hero capturing a major award (or something similar), then it is likewise a good idea to mention that as well.

Once again, this helps the audience appreciate your awareness and concern for their community. It makes them feel that you are one of them, and they can relate to you on a more personal level. It can also help for them to realize, and enjoy, a sense of pride for their community. You will be surprised to learn how this information can help you to find the exact intensity level that you will need to be successful. Knowledge is power, and it is surprising how finding this exact level can help you to exploit the NASCAR Effect throughout the show.

When you're backstage minutes before the show is scheduled to begin, take a moment to listen to the "buzz" coming from the crowd as they enter and take their seats. This noise from the crowd can provide information for you. Is the crowd silent and polite? Does everyone seem ready for a fistfight like after a soccer match between two bitter rival teams? Is the audience chanting or screaming in anticipation? Are there subtleties you can derive from what you hear? You will be surprised how much information is available that will help you to establish the correct intensity level and leverage the NASCAR Effect.

Once again, be in a position to lead the audience from one level of enjoyment to the next. You don't want the audience to lead you and you don't want the audience to become alienated because they cannot relate to you. Remember, it is you who must be in control.

A story about Mark:

As you may know from personal experience, performing in front of a large audience is not something that happens overnight. For most performers, the journey starts at a young age and becomes a career after years of preparation including lessons, collaborations with friends, band rehearsals in the garage, maybe some formal schooling, a lot of paying their dues, and a bit of good fortune.

The following is a story about a performer who tried to get there "the easy way." The purpose of this story is not so much to talk about "the easy way" as it is to explain how not to lead an audience.

There was once a guy named Mark who had a number of odd jobs in his lifetime. Although he had no musical experience or training, he fancied himself as a potential lead singer and he would often sing out loud whenever possible.

At one point in his life, Mark accepted a job as a road manager for a rock band. Mark took this position because he believed it was a first step along his path to fame and fortune. His intentions were to become a star lead vocalist.

During the course of Mark's tenure as a road manager, he continuously demonstrated his singing abilities to everyone within earshot. He sang while driving the bus. He sang during lunch and dinner. He used virtually any opportunity to sing a few lines of a popular song in order to impress the people around him.

At one point, the production company needed to replace the current lead singer. They weren't particularly excited about Mark, but he was available and had been lobbying hard for the position. Due to the time and expense involved in conducting a nation-wide search, the management decided to give Mark a try.

During rehearsals, Mark was a model student. He did everything that was asked of him and he worked hard to learn as much as possible. The management could not imagine the problems that were brewing behind the scenes, though. Unbeknownst to everyone, Mark was plotting to make his first performance the most memorable of all time. Against the intention of his mentors, Mark decided that he would catapult himself to the top… overnight. In doing so, Mark intended to erase any doubts that anyone ever had about his abilities including his own.

Mark's First Show…

Before the start of Mark's first show in front of a real audience, the managers took their seats so they could critique the performance. They were shocked as they witnessed the following:

As soon as the band started playing their first song, Mark immediately ran out into the audience and motioned for everyone to clap along. Since the audience hadn't been prepared for this, no one responded. Not a single person clapped. Instead they all glared at Mark trying to understand what he was doing. Was this a comedy act?

CARDINAL RULE:

Never ask an audience to do something unless you are sure that they are ready and willing to do it.

At this point Mark realized his error and needed to find a way to recover. Instead of simply going back on stage and, somehow finding a way to continue, he started grabbing people's hands and forcing them to clap! The audience collectively rebelled by showing Mark they would not clap under any circumstances. Mark had immediately alienated the entire audience by being insensitive to them and not knowing the appropriate intensity level that should be used at the start of the show.

Let's review some of the things that went wrong.

- Mark did no background checking as to where the audience would be at the start of the show. He did not understand the sophistication level of the audience.

- Mark was not sensitive enough to notice that what he was doing was causing the audience to be alienated.
- Mark didn't have the knowledge or experience to know to stop.

If Mark had been playing to elementary school children, and he had been dressed up as Sponge Bob, his approach may have been perfectly acceptable.

By using Mark as an example, hopefully you will understand that it's extremely important to know your audience and, on an emotion and energy scale, where you should meet them. It would be nice to be able to say that Mark's career eventually improved and that he became a good entertainer, but such is not the case. Mark never did quite understand why things continued to go wrong for him. To this day, Mark continues to dream about getting another break, however, it will most likely never happen. It is best to listen carefully to your mentors and follow their advice as closely as you can. If something goes wrong, try your best to get back on track. Try to learn from your mistakes.

Misjudging the Audience in a Presidential Campaign

Presidential contender Howard Dean made a huge error in 2004 by not appropriately gauging his audience's sophistication level during a famous speech. He was jumping up and down and screaming when his audience was far too sophisticated for such antics. He was the initial forerunner in the Democratic party for the nomination. This over-zealous demonstration has been said to be a large contributing factor in his dropping out of the presidential race. It also provided valuable fodder for late night TV monologues!

Once again, meet your audience where they are. Add a little enthusiasm and intensity to employ the NASCAR Effect. This will allow you to lead the audience through a great journey. If you lead properly, the audience will follow gladly. Otherwise, you could find yourself in an awkward position.

CHAPTER FOUR

ONE-TO-ONE COMMUNICATION

HOW TO DEVELOP A <u>PERSONAL</u> RELATIONSHIP WITH EACH MEMBER OF THE AUDIENCE

Have you ever been to a presentation in a small meeting room where the presenter never looked you in the eye? Such a presenter may have simply explained the information on the overhead slides with no personal interaction whatsoever. In reality, the presenter had given everyone in the room permission <u>not</u> to be involved in the proceedings. Since there was no interaction, the stage was set for people to look at the clock, read ahead in the materials, participate in side discussions, answer mobile phone calls, sleep, etc... On the other end of the spectrum, a presenter who looks at each person in the eye and invites (challenges) each person to become involved will usually find a higher level of engagement, participation and success.

There are a few differences between a performance in a small meeting room and a large concert hall.

Small Meeting Room or Club

- It is easy to see every individual in a small room. In this situation it is very easy to communicate on an individual and personal level.

Large Entertainment Venue

- Due to greater distances between the artist and the audience in a large room, it is difficult, if not impossible, to see the "whites" of people's eyes. The audience sometimes looks like a sea of fuzzy heads.
- You may be able to see clearly the people in the first few rows, but there are other people in the audience who cannot be seen at all. A natural tendency would be to ignore the people you cannot see.
- When the stage lights are bright, you can't see much of anything. You feel like a deer looking into headlights.

The challenge, in larger venues, is to create a scenario that seems as "up close and personal" as that in a small meeting room.

THE ZONE THEORY OF ONE-TO-ONE COMMUNICATION

How to play to an audience of 15,000 people and, after the show, leave each of them feeling as if you had played for each one of them... personally.

Visual Communication

Visual communication, as a part of a successful entertainment process, is much more than simply looking, visually searching or scanning. It is seeing and recognizing. It involves **recognizing** individuals. It is **interactive** and **relational**. It employs the use of physical gestures such as a head nod, a wink, a wave, and many others.

How can you make everyone in the audience feel as if they had been personally played to or communicated with? You've seen great performers like Paul McCartney and Bruce Springsteen going out of their way to shout out to the people in the back, or sing to the top of the stands. They want to make sure that everyone is involved. They know how to communicate with their audience ...**their whole audience**. Here is an amazing way to make everyone feel a part of the show.

Step One: **Section Off the Audience**
Step Two: **Choose a Target Individual in Each Section**
Step Three: **Communicate With Your Target Individuals**
Step Four: **Revisit Your Target Individuals Throughout the Entire Show**

Step One and Two:
SECTION OFF THE AUDIENCE AND SELECT YOUR TARGET INDIVIDUALS

It is obviously impossible to communicate with every individual in a large audience, so you must select a smaller number of people who are strategically selected throughout the room. It is this group of people with whom you will communicate on a "one-to-one" level.

Example: Large concert hall with a balcony. Figure 4 below provides an example of how to divide up an audience of approximately 1,500 people. In this example we will divide the hall or room into 10 sections. *The number of sections will vary depending upon room size, distance from the stage, the presence of a balcony, side sections such as boxes, etc.*

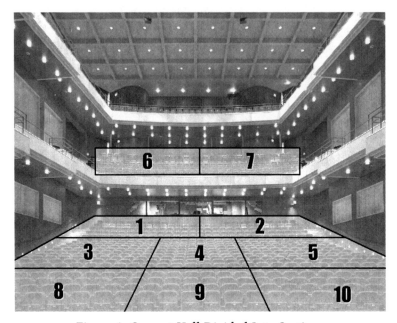

Figure 4: Concert Hall Divided Into Sections

Ideally, you should do your "audience dividing" before the show begins. Why? Because you might find yourself unable to see the audience once you're on stage due to the bright stage lighting. Before the show starts, find a way to peer out into the crowd from a position that renders you virtually invisible. This is important for a number of reasons. For example, you might discover that there is no one in the balcony that night due to light ticket sales. This is good to know before you ask the people in the balcony to sing back to you.

Select an easily detectable person near the center of each section. Remember, in a large hall, it is difficult to see faces from far away, so choose people that are easily distinguishable, perhaps someone with bright red hair or someone wearing a hat or a bright sweater. Choosing a target person in each section is best done at the start of the show. You can only get a potential feel for what the audience will be like before the show, but once the show has started, the audience members come alive and you can make much more informed choices. Try to select people who are conspicuously involved with the show, not the woman who was dragged to the show by her daughter and looks miserable. This will not only help you have a great target person in each section, but it'll also help you keep your intensity level high and your enthusiasm at its best.

Step Three:
VISIT YOUR KEY AUDIENCE MEMBERS

There are two factors affecting the order in which you visit the key members/sections of your audience.

1. **The front sections are free.** Their close proximity to the stage ensures that audience members will be more likely to become and stay engaged in your show. The first few rows of any audience automatically feel a part of your show and feel a bond with you because they're so close to the action!

2. **The rear sections require more attention** since their distance initially makes audience members feel more separated from the stage. These sections will require a more active commitment from the performer(s) throughout the entire show to keep them entertained.

Because of this, it is a smart move to start your show by focusing on the rear of the room. One possible scenario for an order of audience visitation could be the numerical order of the sections in the graphic above. Start at the rear of the room gradually moving forward, then back to the balcony. Due to your close proximity to the front sections, you will automatically have a rapport with them. You can, of course, create your own order of communication. The important point is that the entire room must be covered over and over again throughout the entire show.

Step Four:
CONTINUALLY VISIT YOUR TARGET PEOPLE
THROUGHOUT THE ENTIRE SHOW

Now it's time to shock, surprise and delight them (in other words, make them feel important). As mentioned above, don't start with the front section. They are automatically more involved in the show due to their proximity to the stage. They are the easy ones. You'll visit them later. Pick out your targets in the middle or even in the back of the room. Then... Communicate! You should look directly into the eyes of each person and make some sort of ACTIVE PERSONAL GESTURE (a nod, a wave, a thumbs up, a big smile, etc.) that would convey to him or her that you see them, you like them, and you want them to be your friend and become involved in your party. They might even return your gesture. If they do, you can return the gesture to acknowledge that you saw it and appreciated it. Once you have done this, move to your next target. A word of caution: Make sure you do this in a natural way instead of mechanical. From time to time, you may feel as if it's good to change the order a bit.

Why does this work?

1. When you interact with people in the audience using an active "one-to-one" style of communication, they receive it warmly because you've taken the initiative to enter their world. If you glance at the audience never committing to any eye contact or personal one-to-one communication, you come across as detached and self-absorbed. We've all

seen performers who operate like this (playing to the room or just the band instead of to the <u>people</u> in the room.) Successful one-to-one communication cements the bond between the performer and each audience member.

2. Once you have made the rounds of all of your people in all of the sections, go through the process again. Now you have their attention! They now know that you actually notice them and are taking a personal interest.

3. By the third rotation, you have each person in the palm of your hand. Now they are waiting for you. They have become fully involved in the show, not to mention with you. If you continue doing this, they will stay with you to the very end. They may even ask you for your autograph. As a matter of fact, they probably will.

4. **Don't forget about them and they won't forget about you!**

The Big Secret!

At this point, you may think you have developed a personal relationship with 10 members of the audience, but you're wrong. Depending upon the distance from the stage to each audience section, a significant number of people seated around each of your target members will also feel like they have a personal relationship with you. Why? Here's the secret: Even though you are looking at a specific person, in a specific audience zone, everyone in the immediate vicinity thinks you are looking directly at them. *From a distance of 100 feet, 50 or more people will get the impression that you are communicating with them.* It's simply the way the physics work. You may even want to test this. Go out into the audience and ask a friend to stand on stage and look at a specific seat in your general vicinity but not at you. Walk around the section to find out how far away from the seat you can locate yourself and still get the impression that he is looking directly at you. The larger the room, the greater the effect.

Help! I can't see. The lights are too bright!

What if you scanned the entire audience, sectioned it all off before the start of the show, and you get out on stage and the stage lighting prevents you from seeing anyone in the audience? Should you forget about communicating? No. As a seasoned performer, before the show starts you've surveyed the layout of the room. You know where the seats are, how far they extend, and where the balcony is located. Once you step onto the stage and are blinded by the lights, you should install make-believe friendly audience members in the sections of the audience you cannot see. A good way to do this is to imagine your best friends and relatives seated in those positions. Put Aunt Myrtle up in the balcony, your best friend and college roommate Frank in the middle of the center section, your dog Fang in the balcony, and so forth. Go through the entire process of one-to-one communication with each of your make-believe pals in each section throughout the entire show. At the end of the show you will be met with people you have never seen before, who want to meet you and buy a CD or t-shirt.

"Hold on," you say, won't the audience members be able to tell that you can't see anything? The answer is NO. As long as you naturally <u>simulate</u> the act of communicating one-to-one with a member of the audience, albeit a make-believe member, anyone watching you will believe that you "reached out and touched" them. Why? **What you show them is only what they will see.** A performer is able to create multiple make-believe scenarios with imaginary audience members for the benefit of the audience even though he cannot see past the stage lights. Remember, the audience wants to know that you are interacting with them. You may be acting, but that's show business! The best performers can do this with a sense of natural grace and ease.

HOW TO <u>SPEAK</u> TO AN AUDIENCE USING THE ZONE THEORY OF "ONE-TO-ONE COMMUNICATION"

Have you ever come away from a performance and heard someone saying, "I felt as if the artist was speaking directly to me"? There is a reason for this. The artist used a more intimate "one-to-one" style of speaking to the audience. <u>This ability can be learned, practiced and perfected</u>.

Consider the difference between speaking to one person and speaking to a large room. Which one seems more "up close and personal"? Obviously, speaking with one person is the correct answer. Speaking to a large room has a "shotgun" effect. The words can be heard but, without a personal focus, they impart a lesser degree of sincerity.

To be fair, there are exceptions to every rule. Prince always addresses his audiences in a larger than life way. He speaks to the audience as a whole, but he creates a world of his own that you feel a part of. It's a rock star world in which he delineates himself as the rock star, and lets you know you will be playing the part of the adoring fan. He sets the tone and intensity up front, and then draws you in with his one-to-one communicative skills as a performer.

Stereotypically, human beings tend to respond better to more intimate forms of conversation. Think about Stevie Nicks telling you about a song she wrote during a performance, or Chris Botti introducing a guest performer in his show. To create a more intimate bond with the audience, an artist should speak to them ONE PERSON AT A TIME. The question is, "Who do you speak to?" The answer is, the <u>target persons in the middle of the audience zones</u>.

For example, when you are telling a story or explaining something to the audience, you should begin by looking directly at the person in a zone, as explained above. You speak a few phrases to the first person, move to the second person, and direct a few more phrases to that person. It is best to finish a phrase before moving on to the next person to ensure a natural and personal experience. *The same would hold true for musical phrasing from a lead vocalist or a natural conversation with someone at the dinner table.*

You may know someone who is very personable and engaging in one-on-one communication, but who becomes very impersonal as soon as he/she steps on stage. Such a person may not realize that the same communication skills needed for one-to-one relationships translate perfectly for large crowd situations. Instead of looking aimlessly around the room without focusing on anyone, it's better and more effective to look individual people in the eye and begin an intimate conversation.

Remember:

1. Don't move to the next person until you have completed a phrase or thought.
2. Engage in meaningful communication with individuals.
3. If you can't see people clearly, act as if you can see them perfectly.

SINGING AND PLAYING "ONE-TO-ONE"

As an audience member, would you rather have someone sing or play to the room or to you? The same techniques of one-to-one communication hold true for singers, instrumentalists, and performers of all types. What is more interesting, a guitar player playing while looking at the floor, or a guitar player conspicuously sharing himself and his music with each member of the audience? The ultimate method of performing on stage is sharing everything you do with each member of the audience. If you are feeling dramatic, let it show. If you are feeling elated, don't hide it from your audience. If the music you are creating makes you want to move, then move. Does the song you're performing move you to tears? Joe Cocker sings "You Are So Beautiful" and his voice cracks at the end of the song from emotion. That's incredibly moving. He allowed the audience to share what he was experiencing emotionally. In most cases, the best form of performance is honest and sincere, not plastic and contrived. Most members of the audience are not able to sing or play as well as the performer(s) on stage. Your skill will draw them in, but if you, the performer, allow your feelings to show, a much greater bond can be created and audience members will feel as if they are a part of the performance. You'll get more out of it as well, as you'll be connecting with everyone on a very real basis. They will feel your emotion and intensity. The audience will begin to enter your world.

As a performer, this is not an easy task to accomplish. Many artists are shy, or have a hard time opening up in a real way to anyone, let alone a room of strangers. This fear can be overcome. Think of it as your own personal therapy!

One of the toughest things to do as a songwriter is to write a heartfelt song and have the guts to sing or play it for an audience, thereby exposing a part of you to them. But it is one of the strongest things you can do to endear yourself to an audience. Give them a piece of yourself. Show them something they can't get on a CD. Open up to them. Let your guard down. They won't use it against you.

This concept not only works for one-to-one eye contact and communication, but other aspects of performance as well.

Are you afraid to let them see you sweat? Don't be! After 2+ hours into a Bruce Springsteen show, Bruce took his belt and tightened it to the next notch because he had lost so much weight on stage playing and singing. The audience went wild. The show continued another hour and he made fans for life.

Are you afraid to let the audience see you make faces as you solo or get into your music? Don't be. You're not being awkward, you're doing what you do. Let yourself be swept away by the emotion of playing and singing. Don't be scared to be yourself. You're showing the audience that you're giving your all for them and for your art.

For example, Stevie Wonder rocks back and forth and freely emotes every note he plays when he performs. If he were scared to make movements, no one would ever get to see the real Stevie do his thing. Another example is Jimi Hendrix. He didn't just play the guitar. Hendrix is one of the most influential guitarists in history, but there was more to him than just his playing. He lived it. He meant every note. You could watch his face wince with the pain and ecstasy of the notes he played. His body moved with the music. Jimi's freely displayed intensity and emotion allowed the audiences to share what he was experiencing. You couldn't take your eyes off him....He sucked you into his emotional world.

Employing these concepts will endear you to an audience. If you open up and let the audience into your world as a performer, you will reap what you sow.

STARING DOWN THE BULL

When you make eye contact with someone, it is typically the case that you or the other person will immediately look elsewhere. This is because the act of making eye contact is intimidating. If you allow people to see that someone in the audience intimidates you, it has the effect of making you appear weak or uncommitted. If this happens, the audience will feel your weakness.

Analogies to this exist in the animal world. In certain cases with large animals, the act of showing weakness can be dangerous. One example can be seen at a bullfight. As long as a matador shows bravery in front of the bull and stares the animal down using direct eye contact, he is in the safest possible position. Likewise, if the matador demonstrates fear or intimidation of any kind, he could be in serious trouble. The same is true of a performer. The act of communicating eye-to-eye with a member of the audience and maintaining this direct eye contact is one of the strongest and safest things you can do. It demonstrates your strength and confidence as a performer. Once you practice this form of eye-to-eye communication and become good at it, you will find it to be extremely valuable to your performance.

Remember, the audience has hired you, the artist, to be in charge, to be the "alpha person" for the show. When you initiate eye contact, you express your alpha position. If you are the first to avert your eyes, it will send the confusing message that the audience is the alpha, which is the opposite of what it should be.

What will be the result of this one-to-one style of communication?

1. Everyone around each person you are speaking to will feel like you are speaking directly and personally to them. Think of an audience as one brain composed of many individual cells. Whatever one cell picks up is almost instantaneously transferred to all the surrounding cells.
2. People elsewhere in the audience will sense that you are talking at a personal level to someone in the audience and this will help these audience members empathize and support each other.
3. Your relationship with the entire audience will be strengthened.
4. As you speak throughout the show, you will win over more audience members.
5. You will feel more personally connected to the audience, as you're giving of yourself and connecting on a very real level.
6. Your proficiency in "staring down" will earn you respect. It exudes confidence in yourself and your art. It shows that you are unafraid of sharing who you are and what you do.

CARDINAL RULE:

Never speak, sing or play to a room.
Do all of these to one person at a time.

HOW TO PRACTICE ONE-TO-ONE COMMUNICATION

There is a very good way to practice one-to-one communication. During a rehearsal session or a sound check, practice exactly what you intend to do on stage during a performance. If you plan to play and sing AND create a strong rapport with the audience, you should practice this at every opportunity.

Arrange your rehearsal room to reflect a challenging stage situation

For the aspiring professional, it is a smart idea to practice performing under the most difficult conditions. Create a make-believe audience by imagining the faces of your friends and relatives across the walls in your practice room. Practice while interacting with these faces as you play your music while, at the same time, interacting with your fellow performers. When someone else enters the room, begin interacting with them. Reach out to them as you play to get them involved with what you are doing. In essence, you are urging each person to become involved with you and what you're doing.

Mentally place the audience, the zones, and your target people in the room. Learn to interact with your imaginary audience just like you'd interact with a full house. Communicate with imagined faces on a practice room wall, and you will find it much easier to communicate with an audience when the lights are blinding you. Consider a professional baseball player who swings a weighted bat before stepping up to the plate in order to make the real bat feel lighter and more manageable. A psychological analogy is "stress inoculation." Practice responding automatically to difficult conditions, so that when the difficulty occurs (performing live) you will respond with poise.

THE PLATES SPINNER AT THE CIRCUS

Figure 5: Plate Spinners

For countless years audiences have been amazed and mesmerized by a circus act where the performer spins plates on the top of tall spindles. The plate spinner starts one plate spinning and then, while it is spinning, starts another plate spinning. He continues to add spinning plates while continually revisiting the plates started earlier to ensure that they will not stop spinning and fall off and break. He continues this until he has an amazing number of plates spinning all at the same time. It is an incredible feat to watch. Think of yourself as the plate spinner, the audience members as the plates, and never allow them to fall.

CHAPTER FIVE

THE FLOW OF THE SHOW

HILLS AND VALLEYS

Once you know who you are as an artist, and how to communicate to an audience, you have to contemplate what would make a successful show. Every performer has something they're known for. You need to build your show by focusing on <u>what makes you special</u>. Maybe you're a shredder guitarist. Maybe you're a singer/songwriter and your hit song is a soaring ballad. Build the show from your <u>strengths</u>, but take note that no matter what your artistic style or specialty, if an audience witnesses the same thing over and over, the show will become tedious and boring. Ten soaring ballads later, people will be leaving. Ten shredding guitar solos later, people just aren't as impressed with your speed and agility. After a while, people will glance at their watches and look for the bathrooms. They may enjoy the show but, with no variety or surprises, everything seems to be on autopilot.

A well-crafted show-plan should contain "hills and valleys." Draw on your strengths. Showcase them. But keep in mind that the show elements should be ever changing. If Christina Aguilera just sang riffs and vocal acrobatics all night, the audience would tire of it. They want to hear her sing a melody and deliver a song too. It makes the riffs and vocal acrobatics special when she does sing them. Take your audience on a journey, instead of feeding them the same thing song after song. This concept of "hills and valleys" should propel the show forward and maintain the interest of the audience.

CARDINAL RULE:

A successful, entertaining show must apply and maintain pressure on the audience.

PRESSURE AND DEAD AIR

How is audience pressure created? **Audience pressure is created when the performer's actions on stage compel the audience to become interested and involved.** The audience has no choice but to enter the world of the performer. This situation will maintain itself until the performer allows it to die.

The opposite of pressure during a show is called "Dead Air." **Dead air occurs whenever nothing of interest is happening on stage**. "Dead air" must be avoided at all costs. The effects of dead air are that the audience starts to leave the performer's world and begins considering other concerns:

- The baby-sitter with the kids
- Twitter updates
- The location of the hot dogs and beer
- The best way to get to the parking lot after the show…or should they leave early to avoid the traffic?

One way to think about pressure is to remember the best movie you ever saw in a movie theater. Remember how the movie hooked you and transported you to a new world? Most likely you stayed in this new world until the movie was over and the lights came on. You transitioned back into your own world as the dead air filled the theater once the movie was over. You might have even mentioned afterwards that the time seemed to pass quickly.

The psychological concept of "flow" is relevant here. The pressure is actually a *challenge* that the audience has joined with the artist. The challenge is to participate with the artist in creating something moving. No challenge = bored; too much challenge = overwhelmed. Just the right amount of challenge or pressure = flow. When we say "keep the pressure on the audience," we're basically saying "keep them engaged in this challenging creation."

Unlike a Movie, a Stage Performance Requires Interaction

A major difference between a movie and a stage performance is the potential for real-time, human interaction between the performer(s) and the members of a live audience. In order for the audience to leave their world and join yours, you must interact. In fact, it's like a pendulum swinging. It's all a matter of elementary physics. Below is an explanation that is crafted specifically for all of the physicists who feel compelled to read this book. For the rest of us, take note, as this might be the first time ever that performance and physics have been mentioned together and likened to each other!

PERFORMANCE AND THE LAWS OF PHYSICS

PHYSICS LESSON 1:
NEWTON'S FIRST LAW OF MOTION

Newton's first law of motion states that "An object at rest tends to stay at rest and an object in motion tends to stay in motion with the same speed and in the same direction unless acted upon by an unbalanced force." Objects "tend to keep on doing what they're doing." In fact, it is the natural tendency of objects to resist changes in their state of motion. This tendency to resist changes in their state of motion is described as inertia.

Inertia = the resistance an object has to a change in its state of motion.

Translation: An audience will remain disinterested until you do something that interests them. Some audiences are more difficult than others and, thus, require more effort on the part of the performer to attract their interest.

PHYSICS LESSON 2:
FORCE AND ITS REPRESENTATION

A force is a push or pull upon an object resulting from the object's *interaction* with another object. Whenever there is an *interaction* between two objects, there is a force upon each of the objects. When the *interaction* ceases, the two objects no longer experience the force. Forces <u>only</u> exist as a result of an interaction.

Translation: A compelling performance and an involved audience is a powerful experience to behold. If the performance ceases to be compelling, this amazing experience ceases to exist.

PHYSICS LESSON 3:
NEWTON'S THIRD LAW OF MOTION

A force is a push or a pull upon an object that results from its interaction with another object. Forces result from interactions!

"For every action, there is an equal and opposite reaction."

Translation: If you come on stage exhibiting energy, the audience's level of energy will tend to follow yours. Example: If you smile at them, they will tend to smile back at you.

AUDIENCE PRESSURE

An audience files in and sits down in a passive state. They will remain in this state until someone exerts pressure on them. For instance:

1. Someone yells "Fire!"
2. A knowledgeable, experienced artist or group walks onto the stage and instantly engages the audience on a personal, one-to-one level employing well-performed entertainment at the appropriate intensity level, and by using the NASCAR Effect, and takes them on a journey allowing them to enter the artist's world with little or no "dead air."

THE BALLOON ANALOGY

One way to explain the word "pressure" within the context of a performance is to use the example of inflating a balloon.

The show is the balloon. The air is the pressure. It must be blown up and kept properly inflated.

A balloon with very little or no air in it is flabby and virtually useless. When a balloon contains air, it can be used effectively for a number of useful purposes. Moreover, when a balloon is properly inflated to it's capacity and has an explosive nature, it has the ability to captivate the attention of everyone present. In a show context, pressure does not necessarily relate to tempo or loudness. A band can play a dramatic, slow song that can produce a great deal of pressure. Pressure here relates to the bond that you create and hold with the audience.

The trick is to inflate the balloon, release a little from time to time (hills and valleys), and continue to blow air into the balloon without allowing <u>most</u> of the air to escape. If, for some reason, you were to let <u>all</u> the air out of the balloon (dead air) you would need to restart the process from the beginning to re-inflate the balloon.

This analogy holds true when considering a performance. If there is no pressure (no air in the balloon) placed on an audience, a performance will have little impact. The audience must work to remain interested, and eventually they will tire of it. A performance with little or no pressure would be categorized more as background music. There is nothing to keep you as an audience member engaged. You could just go buy the CD and listen in your home and have the same experience.

When the pressure is strong, it is relatively easy to keep the audience captivated. The bond you have created with your audience is powerful. This is like sailing a sailboat with plenty of wind. The boat becomes very easy to steer. Without wind, a sailboat goes nowhere. When a show is stagnant (no air in the balloon), the audience may be tempted to:

- Buy a Coke
- Look for a bathroom
- Check facebook
- Talk to a friend
- Or worse…get up and leave

Good Pressure (Inflated Balloon):

- Something compelling is happening on stage
- The performer looks excited to be here
- The performer put some thought into how he/she looks (The look is interesting, distinctive and attention grabbing)
- The performer is talking with/to the audience
- The performer is working very hard on stage
- The energy on stage is being directed toward and for the benefit of the audience
- The show is properly paced with well-executed "hills and valleys"
- The show contains surprises leaving the audience wondering what will come next
- There is movement on stage
- The audience is applauding
- The performer is graciously receiving applause
- The performer is paying compliments to the audience

Pressure Leaks (Deflated Balloon):

- Nothing is happening on stage – dead air
- Waiting too long during the downward slope of the

applause cycle (applause cycles will be discussed in a later chapter) before beginning the next part of the show
- Standing with your back to the audience
- Inside jokes on stage
- The performer looks disinterested
- The performer looks like just another person off the street
- The performer checks the time on his watch
- The performer pays no compliments to the audience
- The performer is interacting with someone else on stage and ignoring the audience
- The performer stands too far in the background or takes steps backward
- The performer walks out of the lights
- No one-to-one communication is taking place
- The performer is making unnecessary adjustments to equipment and seems preoccupied, rather than engaged with the audience or show

SHOW PACING: SONG LEVELS

Before launching into the subject of show pacing, it is important to mention the concept of a "set." A "set" is simply a collection of songs that are chosen in order to achieve a successful result by virtue of the individual song qualities and their effective placement within the show.

A successful show should contain songs that run the gamut with regard to style, tempo and intensity. If every song in the show were to be the same vibe, tempo, in the same key, and the same level of intensity, the audience would soon become bored. **Predictability Kills!** Therefore, the flow of the show must be carefully paced. If you instantly change from the lowest intensity song to the highest intensity song, and then back to a low intensity song, the audience would feel a bit lost and even frustrated. This is an example of <u>not</u> using the NASCAR Effect. The pacing in a show must ebb and flow with thoughtful communication and well-planned song choices, all by the intelligent design of you, the artist. Therefore, it is a good idea to insert songs into your set using a song intensity scale as a tool. A song intensity scale from 1 to 5 (1 being the most mellow and 5 being the most energetic and intense) works well.

Level 1:   This is the least energetic song level. This category would include sensitive ballads but not power ballads. A Level 1 song has a slow, easy tempo. Hard, abrupt, well-defined rhythm would not be a characteristic of this category of song. Intimacy would more likely be a characteristic.

A Level 1 song is never a starting place for a set. It is a great place from which to build energy upwards in the middle of a set. It can also serve as a comfortable point on which to land after a particularly intense, hard driving section of a show. In other words, welcome relief.

Examples: "Beautiful" by James Blunt, "Philadelphia" by Bruce Springsteen, "Angel" by Sara McLachlan, "Like A Star," by Corinne Bailey Rae

Level 2:   This is one notch upward from Level 1. It has more energy and more of a beat, but still maintains a comfortable slower pace. Power ballads might fit into Level 2. You can slow dance to a Level 2 song.

Examples: "No More Drama" by Mary J Blige, "Waiting on the World to Change" by John Mayer, "Faithfully" by Journey, "Better Together" by Jack Johnson

Level 3: This is a medium paced song, not hard driving or aggressive. It is typically a transitional song, or stepping stone, occupying an energy-building portion of the set.

Examples: "Rock Your Body" by Justin Timberlake, "Brown Sugar" by The Rolling Stones, "My Humps" by The Black-Eyed Peas, "Need You Now" by Lady Antebellum

Level 4: A Level 4 song is a relatively urgent, high-energy song that typically would make people want to dance or move. It is a song played during a higher energy portion of the set. Typically, you would play a couple of Level 4 songs in a row to allow the audience to get more energetically involved in the set. A Level 4 section of the set should last just long enough to give the audience a good workout, but should change to a different energy level, usually low, at a moment when the audience is getting tired.

Examples: "Hollaback Girl" by Gwen Stefani, "Beautiful Day" by U2, "Rolling In the Deep" by Adele, "Rebel, Rebel" by David Bowie

Level 5: A Level 5 song is one of the major peaks of the show. It is at the top of the energy/intensity scale. A level 5 song is typically used at the end of a long energy build and/or as a show closer. There is nowhere higher to go after a Level 5 song. It is typically one of the most well-known and/or well-loved songs to the audience. It's one of the songs they specifically came to hear, and it is also a song that is usually impossible to follow.

Examples: "Crazy In Love" by Beyonce, "1999" by Prince, "Use Somebody" by Kings of Leon, "Satisfaction" by The Rolling Stones, or "Born To Run" by Bruce Springsteen

CARDINAL RULE:

The two most important songs in a concert are the opener and the closer.

THE SHOW OPENER

What type of song should you choose for the show opener? The show opener is your introduction to the audience. It is during the show opener that they get their first look/impression of you and begin to form opinions about whether or not they like you. This is NOT the time to make your ultimate artistic statement. It is your first opportunity to begin bonding with the audience. This is the initial point of contact where you need to firmly establish your character and image. As a paragraph has an opening sentence that sets the stage for what is said and contained in the paragraph, so your first song sets the stage for what is to come in your show.

The show opener should:

- Be a "feel good" song that requires very little intense, artistic concentration on the part of the audience
- Have a good amount of energy to bring the audience from a waiting state to an involved state
- Set the tone for the entire show
- Give the audience a great idea of who you are as an artist

Using Physical Properties to Help with the Show Opener
The following is a story that took place many years ago that involves a world-class sound engineer as he was preparing for the sound check in a very large concert hall:

He was spending a great deal of time adjusting the sound of the bass drum. Although the sounds coming from the bass drum seemed somewhat similar, from one beat to another, there were, in fact, subtle differences. One extreme was a "boomy" sound. The other extreme was more of a "popping" sound. When the sound level for the bass drum was finally captured, somewhere in between a boom and a pop, he was asked why he spent so much time on this seemingly trite exercise. His answer was surprising. He explained that he was trying very hard to simulate the sound and feel of a human heartbeat. If he could make a beat of the bass drum sound and feel like a human heart, then the people in the audience would hear and feel the same thing. If this happened, their heartbeats would try to adjust to the much louder beat of the bass drum. The sound engineer and the band had collaborated on an effective way to start the show. The collaboration effort went something like this:

1. The bass drum was adjusted to sound like a human heart.
2. The band would come on stage and begin playing a song with a tempo that is slightly faster than that of a human heart.

3. The result would be that the audience members' heart beats increased slightly in order to catch-up to the sound of the bass drum. When this happened, each member of the audience would feel an instant rush of adrenaline for purely physiological reasons.

THE SHOW CLOSER

The show closer must be the exclamation point at the end of the show. The last song is you and your audience's last opportunity to reach the biggest peak that will be attained. This is the song to bring them to their feet. It's the big celebration song. It's the song they all know and love. It's the song that they never want to end, and it will leave them wanting more.

SHOW PACING EXAMPLES

The following example includes numbered song values along with the methodology for choosing them. This is just an example of an interesting set, not a template for every set.

1. **Show Opener:** Level 4 Song – Begin at a good energy level and get the audience going. The audience is checking you out.
2. Level 4 song – Keep it going and let them know you intend to create an up, fun atmosphere.
3. Welcome to the audience – "We're glad to be here. You people are great!"
4. Level 3 song – Medium intensity song to comfortably get things going again while providing room to build.
5. Level 3.5 song – Not too intense yet, but we're adding a little energy.
6. Level 4 song – Yeah! Now you've got it moving.

7. Level 4 song –Yeah, let's keep it up! You've still got it moving. By the end of this song the show has been moving at an up-tempo pace for enough time that the audience might need a change. At the end of this song, hit the last big staccato chord to end it and the very next beat goes all the way down to the low-key downbeat of a Level 1 song.

8. Level 1 song – Beautiful, intimate, mellow song. A great change of pace after the long string of higher energy songs. In effect, you have set the audience up for a surprise. You have built them up and then pulled the rug out from underneath them, leaving them in a beautiful place of comfort and rest. If you work this one right you will get good applause.

9. Level 2.5 song – You're starting to move upward again.

10. Level 3.5 Song – Build up with a medium song.

11. Level 4 Song – It's time to start to build a peak again.

12. Level 4 Song – Keep it going!

13. Time for an energy rest for the audience. The front person compliments the audience and introduces the members of the band.

14. Level 3 Song – Get it going again.

15. Level 3.5 Song – Give it more energy.

16. Level 4 Song – You're rocking again.

17. Level 4 Song – Keep it up! Move the audience towards the peak of the show.

18. **Level 5 Song – Show Closer:** During the introduction of this Level 5 song, the front person breaks down the band and tells the audience that he or she and the band have had an incredible time. This has been one of the best audiences they have ever played for, and this will be the last song. It also happens to be the song they've been waiting for. As soon as the song intro begins, the audience becomes ecstatic! You milk this song for all it's worth. Everybody in the audience is going crazy, and

everybody on stage is dripping wet with sweat. The audience is overwhelmed with excitement and joy. Finally, after you've done everything possible with this song, you set up and play a gigantic trashcan ending that lasts for a long time. The front person finally cuts off the chord with a grandiose gesture, takes one step forward toward the audience, flashing a big smile while holding his hands out to the side with his palms upward. The audience jumps out of their seats, or if they were already standing during the song, they remain standing for a **STANDING OVATION**!

Two More Show Pacing Examples

Here are two examples of show pacing and how they might look if a chart method were used.

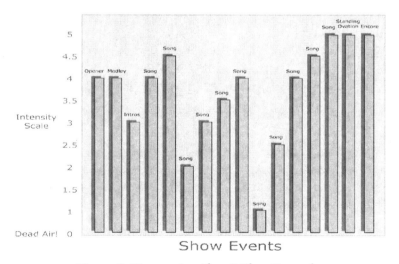

Figure 6: "Interesting Show" Flow Example

The chart above illustrates a carefully created show flow geared toward beginning, establishing and maintaining a show experience that will retain the audience's interest from start to finish.

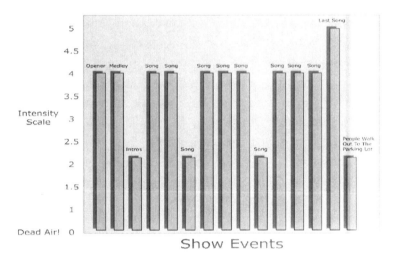

Figure 7: "Boring Show" Flow Example

This chart illustrates a show flow that is too predictable and thus, boring. The audience will soon tire of a show containing few surprises and become bored. The outcome will be people who can't wait to get out into the parking lot and drive away after the show. The possibility of an encore is doubtful.

Don't be a glorified jukebox where there is no plan or intention to take the audience anywhere in particular. Live performance should take an audience on a journey. There are musical genres where show flows differ from the normal "rules," such as trance or electronica, but as a general rule, create a journey that allows the audience members to enjoy moments of:

- Emotional ups-and-downs
- Comedy
- Sentiments
- Personal reflection
- Surprise

SET LISTS ARE NO ACCIDENT

Check out these iconic bands and the set lists they chose. Are they interesting? Are there hills and valleys? Do they take you on a journey? You bet!

The Rolling Stones
March 4, 2006 Las Vegas NV
MGM Grand Garden Arena

Jumpin' Jack Flash 5
It's Only Rock 'n' Roll 4
Let's Spend the Night Together 3
Oh No, Not You Again 3
Tumbling Dice 2
Beast of Burden 1-2
Bitch 4
Midnight Rambler 4
Gimme Shelter 5
This Place Is Empty 2
Happy 5
Miss You 3-4
Rough Justice 3
You Got Me Rocking 4
Honky Tonk Woman 4
Sympathy For The Devil 4
Start Me Up 4
Brown Sugar 5
You Can't Always Get What You Want 2-3-4 (first half song=2, second half=3 or 4)
Satisfaction 5

No Doubt
6/13/04 Chicago IL
Tweeter Center

Just A Girl 4
Excuse Me Mr. 4
Ex-Girlfriend 4
Underneath It All 3
Hey Baby 4
Bathwater 3.5
Running 2
Simple Kind of Life (acoustic) 2
Hella Good 4
New 4
Don't Speak 5
It's My Life 3
Spiderwebs 4
Sunday Morning 5

If you were to compare artist set lists for multiple concerts, you would find that the set lists are usually fairly similar from one show to the next. The reason for this might be that the band or artist has found that this particular order of songs works most of the time (100% Rule).

If you'd like to check out set lists for other artists go to http://www.setlist.com. You can compare and contrast popular artists whose songs are familiar to you, and study how they build their set lists.

WATCH YOUR TEMPOS

It is very common for performers to be so anxious about the show that their anxiety can be detected in overly fast song tempos. There is a lot of adrenaline present in a live situation that can create an excitement on the part of the performer that can create this need for speed. If a band were to compare the tempos from a live performance with the tempos of the original recordings, they might be surprised. In some cases the tempos are so fast in the live performances that the songs are hardly recognizable. As a general rule, song tempos should be a few beats per minute (BPM) faster live than on the CD, because live performance does create more energy, but the songs should still be recognizable and provide the same musical feel as the record performance if you're performing the same arrangement as the record.

It's very important for the leaders, and especially the drummers, to establish the tempos and hold the band members to it. Other group members may push, and even fight unknowingly, to make the tempo faster. The adrenaline of playing live usually makes musicians want to push the tempos without even realizing it. <u>Be aware!</u> Even though this pushing is taking place, it is important to hold steady.

For years, many well-known performing acts have provided a click-track to their drummers by way of an earpiece that fits snugly into one, or both, ears. This click-track has properly spaced clicks that help the drummer know the correct tempo for the song. This click-track can be enormously helpful when the venue is filled with excited fans. Musicians can get caught up in this excitement and speed tempos up and up and up without thinking. <u>Keep it steady!</u>

A strong reason for maintaining the proper tempo is as follows: The tempo for a song was initially established because it worked best with rhythmically timed elements that encouraged listeners to react. For example, a song with a funky beat is arranged to make people want to move and dance. In many cases it's not so much the musical notes as much as it is the empty spaces between the notes that affects the listener. When tempos are too fast, the musical stimuli and the empty spaces are altered in such a manner that the effect is now different. In fact, a funky song can be turned into a wall of ineffective noise when the tempo becomes too fast.

THE GAUGE OF LIFE AND DEATH

At any given point during a show, you are either living or dying. It is not the audience's choice. It is your choice. When selecting songs for a set, be aware that your choices will have an effect on the pacing of the show and ultimately whether you live or die on stage. Some songs may be perfect on the album, but might not get a strong reaction in a live concert situation. Be sensitive to this and be able to axe or adjust the arrangement to a song that, for some reason, isn't translating to your audience in a live setting. Keep in mind that your set list can be changed during the show, as you gauge your audience's responses. **Setlists are made to be broken.** You have the power to live or die by these moment-to-moment changes. Be sensitive to "The Gauge of Life or Death." Choose "Life." See Figure 8 below.

The Gauge of Life or Death

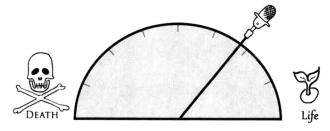

Figure 8: The Gauge of Life or Death

Song selection can:

1. Increase show pressure
- Faster tempo
- More popular song
- Louder song

2. Decrease show pressure
- Slower tempo
- Less popular song
- Quieter song
- Boring song
- Extended soloing with limited appeal to the audience

3. Maintain the current pressure level
- Similar tempo
- Similar style

4. Inject more fun
- Audience involvement – Sing-a-longs, "Let me hear you scream!" etc.
- Playing an audience's favorite song

- Play your version of a cover song the audience wouldn't expect from you

5. Cause less fun
- Playing too many similar songs in a row

6. Surprise the audience – Surprises are good. They keep the audience awake and alert.
- A song with a radical change in tempo or energy. For instance, after a build to a high, energy peak you pull the rug out from underneath the audience and begin playing a very soft, sensitive song that the audience loves. At first they are shocked but then become pleased by your clever manipulation of music choices.

7. Create boredom
- No changes (stylistic, energy, tempo) for a long time
- Play songs that the audience doesn't relate to

CHAPTER SIX

STAGE MOVEMENT AND AWARENESS

ALWAYS BE AWARE OF WHAT IS HAPPENING ON STAGE. IT'S NOT ALWAYS ABOUT YOU; IT'S ABOUT THE ENTIRE STAGE INCLUDING EVERYONE AND EVERYTHING THAT'S ON IT.

WHY MOVE ON STAGE?

There is an old show biz saying that **audiences hear with their eyes**. This is true to a large degree since most members of an audience are not musically educated to a large enough degree to be able to intelligently deduce the level of artistic quality of the performer. For this reason, performers have historically used many extra forms of assistance to ensure success with audiences:

- Flashy show clothes
- Massive stacks of guitar and bass amplifiers
- Powerful stage lighting
- Pyrotechnics
- **Lots of movement on stage**

One of the most successful forms of entertainment in history has been the three-ring circus. Three large rings were set up across the floor, each with a totally different act in progress. The audience didn't know where to look next. If they looked at ring number one they would miss the activities in the other two rings and vice versa. This made for an exciting experience that kept them coming back for more.

EFFECTIVE STAGE MOVEMENT
If you want to attract and hold an audience's attention, movement helps.

Side-to-Side vs. Front-to-Back

Performance involves movement, which occurs with two basic types: Side-to-side and front-to-back. Which type do you believe is preferable from an audience's perspective? The answer is side-to-side.

Side-to-side, or lateral, movement is easier to detect from the audience. Sometimes, when a performer is moving forward or backward, a person seated further back in the audience cannot detect any movement at all. This is easy to test. Ask a friend to stand about 50 feet away from you and move front-to-back and then side-to-side. You will notice that side-to-side movement is far easier to detect from a distance. This is important, since you want your audience to feel a part of every movement and gesture on stage. If they can't see it, they can't react to it. Taking this concept farther, moving from one side of the stage to the other and back again creates a much greater effect than moving from the front to the back of the stage.

The following is a story that illustrates the value of lateral movement:

Jeff learned about stage movement the hard way. He routinely dripped with sweat from constant movement; however, the audience came away with the impression that he never moved at all! People would ask him why he'd simply stand in one place throughout the show. This contradiction was so frustrating to Jeff that he had to find the answer. He asked a professional to critique his performance and tell him how it could be true that he moved so much, and worked so hard, but nobody would notice or react. The professional told Jeff that his movements were all front-to-back. A person in the audience does not have much depth perception. Side-to-side movements are more noticeable. In the end, Jeff learned how to make a much bigger impression on the audience by incorporating more side-to-side movements in his show. An added bonus was that he no longer needed to work as hard!

How Large Should My Movements Be?

Large Venue

Should your movement on a large stage be the same as your movement on a small stage? The answer is no. On a large stage the venue is typically large, meaning there are more people in the audience. Many of these people are seated far away from the stage. Therefore, movement, gestures and facial expressions on stage should be exaggerated or amplified to be more detectable from a distance. Carefully exaggerated movement on a large stage looks normal to the audience seated at a distance.

Small Venue

Movement on a small stage, which is typically found in a smaller venue, should be appropriate for the size of the room. Smaller venues and their stages provide a much more intimate atmosphere with nearly everyone in the audience being able to clearly see the performers. In this type of situation facial expressions are easier to see. Movement that would work on a large stage can look overdone on a smaller stage.

Always adjust your movements with the audience in mind. Make sure they feel a part of the show by matching your movements to the size of the venue.

Move With The Music

Well-played music has "feel." Many musicians feel their music physically. They have a natural tendency to move as they play their parts. In fact, if you were to ask them to stand still while playing they would feel hampered. They physically want to move as part of their playing style. It adds feel to their music. A by-product of this physical feel is that it tends to affect the audience in the same way. Members of the audience will feel the music and want to move to it. It's a cause and effect. Great musicians, who are moving as they are adding feel to their music, are also much more interesting to watch from an audience perspective.

You can take this concept even further by not just moving to the beat, but accenting important beats and changes in the song by changes in your motion. James Brown, the "Godfather of Soul" would fall to the ground when he would "break down" a section. It was dramatic. His actions made the audience know a few things, (1) that he was in control of where the music was going, (2) that he was dedicated to and in the moment of every beat of his music, (3) that the audience should feel a change of emotion during this next section of the song.

You've seen artists pump the microphone into the air as they have the audience sing or chant a part of their song. This is a great example of using effective movement to your advantage.

You're interacting, you're directing, and you're extending your energy towards your audience. This will always work!

Movement vs. No Movement

Be aware of what your movement portrays. If you've been jumping around the stage for a few songs, and you bring the level down for a ballad, move appropriately for that ballad. Sometimes, after a lot of movement for a number of songs, it's incredibly powerful to stand in one place for a few moments and deliver a ballad. You can captivate people by not moving at all, if it's done in the right manner, and with attention to your changes in motion on different songs and moods.

Visual Tools to Critique Movement

You would be well advised to film your movement on stage in both large and small venues. This should give you an accurate appraisal of the effectiveness of your onstage movement. A picture is worth a thousand words.

Band Interaction

You may be a stand-up comic and be the only one on stage to interact with and communicate to the audience. Your movements may be all the audience has to hold on to and bring them to different points in your show. Be aware of that. However, you may be part of a band or group onstage. Everyone's movements in a band can add or detract from your show.

Practice Moving and Playing/Singing

If you are not used to moving while playing or singing you should practice doing so in order to develop the ability to be comfortable and natural on stage. Practice playing or singing your parts while moving around the room. Also, practice playing in uncomfortable positions until they become more comfortable. Practice while standing on boxes or chairs. Practice jumping off of things. Practice in situations where there are many things to divert your attention from what you're doing. In other words, practice moving to extremes while playing and singing in order to become more comfortable, fluid and natural under normal circumstances. It might seem weird at first, but after thirteen or so times it will feel more natural.

ONSTAGE INTERACTION AND ONE-TO-ONE AUDIENCE COMMUNICATION

Now that you know that movement is an important part of your show, you need to decide whom that movement will be directed toward. There are no hard and fast rules here. It's most natural to mix it up. For example, Steven Tyler of Aerosmith may start out a song singing directly into the audience, using one-to-one communication. He may move eventually to Joe Perry, the lead guitarist, and interact with him for a while, and then they both might move back to a more one-to-one communication with the audience. Interaction between band-mates is natural and it lets the audience know that you're a team. If you just sing or play only into the audience all night, it will become boring, just as if you played songs of the same tempo all night. Interact. You can draw attention toward certain band members at opportune moments in the song, and you can create a feeling of camaraderie that the audience can feel a part of.

CARDINAL RULE:

Always support what is happening onstage.

You have the power to direct people's attention towards what you want them to focus on. Use that to your advantage.

If someone on stage is doing something special such as speaking to the audience or taking a solo, intently direct your attention toward that person so that audience members will have their attention re-directed from you to the speaker or soloist. Always direct your audience members where to look. Don't misdirect your audience's attention and dilute their enthusiasm. They will follow your lead wherever you take them.

MISDIRECTION

Misdirection is a no-no, and takes away from the flow and pressure of the show. A common term for this misdirection is "upstaging."

Misdirection involves doing something on stage that tends to distract the audience from the main point of focus. Magicians commonly use misdirection to their advantage to cause their audience to look elsewhere while they make a secret move. Magicians know that misdirection can be extremely subtle and still cause the entire audience to look away. In a stage performance, it takes only a small bit of misdirection to send the entire audience looking to the wrong place.

For example, a musician may take a moment to look at his or her wristwatch during a part in the show. Where do you think the entire audience will be looking? They will be looking at the performer's wristwatch. That's right! You will have 15,000 people either looking at the performer's wristwatch or their own wristwatch instead of enjoying the show. Are you watching someone walk out of the theater as you talk to the audience? Be assured that if you do, the whole audience will watch them too. You have that much power over your audience's actions and reactions.

Another important psychological aspect of this is that the audience members will look to a supporting artist or sideman on stage as a guide for what they should be feeling about the solo or the performer featured at the time. It helps tremendously for the supporting members on stage to act as a model, or emote the feelings that they would like the audience to have. For example, it makes a huge difference if a supporting artist rolls his eyes vs. looks with excitement at what the featured performer is doing. Every move you make and feeling you convey on stage is reflected by the audience, whether you want it to be or not.

I recently saw one of my favorite jazz artists perform in a small club. One of the most alluring parts of a jazz performance is the soloing, as improvisation is a huge part of any jazz concert-going experience. As excited as I was at the beginning of the show, by the second or third solo, I was bored. The soloists were incredible and world class. However, everyone else on the stage appeared so unfazed by it all that it took the joy out of it for me.

As I listened to one of the most incredible piano solos of the night, I looked at the saxophonist and he was staring at the ceiling bored, as if he was in math class. He could have at least looked interested. It detracted from the solo and the show. Remember that even if you're not the featured performer at a particular moment, you're still on stage. The lights are on and people can see you.

Try your best to be aware of what **you** are doing so you don't detract from the focus of what is being presented on stage. Add and/or complement what is going on through your movements, gestures and facial expressions.

Unintentional Misdirection

Occasionally you will see musicians take care of a technical matter during someone else's solo. A good example is a guitar player using the drum solo time as an opportunity to change a guitar string (without leaving the stage). The original thought of waiting until something else is happening to take care of a technical matter that should be taken care of out of the spotlight is correct. Although the guitar player thinks he's doing the right thing, the majority of the audience will be watching the guitar player changing his string. This unfortunate display of misdirection will captivate the crowd and cheat the drummer out of an opportunity to mesmerize the audience. It is far better to change the guitar string off-stage or even better, pick up a spare guitar that is sitting there for this very situation.

Intentional Misdirection

Every rule is made to be broken, and as stated at the top of this book, there are no hard and fast rules that can never be broken. At Coachella recently, Marcus, the lead guitarist for Mumford and Sons, broke a string. He's known for breaking strings. It's happened more than a few times in the middle of huge concert events, and he's a seasoned pro. He tried to divert the attention away from himself by telling another band member to play a song while he changed strings. But every camera was on Marcus and his guitar, as the audience intently watched. No one was budging. He made the most of it, and everyone cheered wildly as he changed his string in record time and started the next song flawlessly. It was almost as if it was a part of the act.

MAINTAIN STAGE BALANCE

What happens when one person moves to another position on the stage and leaves his former spot empty? If a stage position is left empty or unprotected, audience coverage can suffer. Whenever a performer moves to a different position on stage, someone should take his place to prevent that section of the audience from feeling neglected. For example, if most of your band ends up on one end of the stage at a certain point in the song, who is communicating from the other side of the stage? In a perfect world, all of the performers should cover all of the stage positions and communicate with the entire audience at all times. And if you all end up on one side of the stage together, make sure you make it an event and communicate to the entire audience during that event, knowing that you must regain your stage balance quickly.

STAGE AWARENESS

Always be aware of what is going on around you. Just as if you were driving a car, know who and what surrounds you. It's helpful to know if the bass player is moving backwards to cue a section of the song so you don't get hit in the head with the neck of the bass. It's also helpful to know who is where on stage, so you can maintain proper audience coverage and stage balance. Many unfortunate things can occur during a performance, not only to you, but also to your fellow performers. Cymbal stands can fall over. Drum mics can move out of place. Guitar cables can become entangled or can get pulled so tightly that people may trip over them on stage. Mic stands can lower by themselves. If you remain aware and you notice a problem like this, you can (1) avoid getting caught up in it, (2) you can help by fixing it with ease and grace, or (3) you can call it to the attention of a roadie or a stage tech. <u>Be aware</u>. It helps everyone.

CHAPTER SEVEN

APPLAUSE AND APPLAUSE CYCLES

THE AUDIENCE AND THEIR PAROCHIAL TRAINING

Fortunately, performers everywhere can count on crowds having years of audience schooling beginning with kindergarten. Our teachers and principals taught us to:

- Stand in a line
- Be attentive when an authority figure is talking
- Stand-up when instructed
- Sit down
- Clap
- Make noise
- Hush up

A performer is correct in assuming that an audience is fully prepared to follow along as instructed. This assumption is relevant in many places around the world where school systems are particularly strict. People remain responsive to these signals for a lifetime. This schooling can work in favor of the performer, and it can also work against him.

Common gestures such as extending your arms and holding your palms upward can signal to the audience that applause is welcome. The inverse is also true. Palms held downward typically signify that it is time to shush up.

You may want to capture, in your mind's eye, the following scenario:

You are seated in a quiet auditorium and the stage is completely empty except for a small podium centered in front of the stage. A man walks onto the stage and steps directly in front of the podium. The man does not say a word; however, he extends his arms with his palms up slowly. He nods his head to the audience as if to say, "Please stand up."

Everyone stands up.

You can imagine the reverse being true when the same man wants you to sit down. Smart, experienced performers take advantage of this parochial training and use it to their benefit.

APPLAUSE AND THE CHRISTMAS STORY

The best analogy I know regarding applause is the giving of gifts during Christmastime. Applause from an audience is a gift just like any other.

John and Mary spend a great deal of time prior to the annual Christmas party buying presents for the employees who work at their firm. They go out of their way to purchase and wrap gifts that are perfectly suited for each co-worker. As soon as they arrive at the Christmas party, they immediately find opportunities to greet their co-workers and present their gifts. They start out by cornering Marvin, a Vice President of Sales & Marketing. As they hand Marvin his beautifully wrapped gift, Marvin motions (with his hands) that he really doesn't deserve it. He appears to be very pleased and flattered, however, he doesn't accept the gift. **John and Mary feel rejected.**

After Marvin, John and Mary focus their attention on Trina in the Human Resources department. John and Mary have trouble giving their gift, as Trina is laughing and joking around with a friend. It's difficult to get her attention. John and Mary become frustrated and leave in order to find another co-worker. **John and Mary once again feel rejected and unimportant.**

John and Mary then find Charles from the Accounts Receivables department. They try their best to give Charles his gift; however, Charles is talking non-stop and won't shut-up. They can't seem to make Charles understand that they're trying to give him a gift. **Again, John and Mary feel rejected and unimportant.**

Finally, John and Mary locate Stephanie from the Public Relations department and present her with their gift. As soon as Stephanie sees the gift, she stops everything and expresses her delight and gratitude. Stephanie is very gracious as she accepts the gift with enthusiasm and humility. Stephanie then surprises John and Mary with a carefully wrapped gift. **John and Mary feel appreciated.**

As you can see, the relationship between the audience and the performers is of utmost importance. John and Mary giving their gifts represent the audience giving their gifts of applause. The performers are the co-workers either accepting or not accepting the gifts. In real life, a performer's analogy would be:

Upon hearing about a music group performing in the area, loyal fans purchase tickets in order to attend an up-coming concert. On the specified date, the performers arrive and the audience files into the concert hall. The show starts. After the first song, the audience responds by clapping and expressing their enthusiasm and appreciation. Instead of responding with gratitude, one performer makes motions to shush the audience (like

Marvin). A second performer tells an inside joke to a fellow band member (like Trina). A third performer jabbers nonstop into the microphone (like Charles). From here on, the audience will be polite and make the best of the situation. It is doubtful that many people in the audience will feel a personal connection to the band and feel compelled to buy their album or another ticket to their next show.

Compare the response with this scenario:

The music group stands onstage visually receiving the applause with a look of sincere appreciation. As the applause begins to die down, the spokesman for the group thanks the audience as if it is the first time they have ever received such a wonderful response. The audience begins to clap louder as a relationship is developing. The relationship now surprises and inspires the audience. The group and the audience can start taking their new relationship to the next level.

CARDINAL RULE:

Never underestimate the importance and value of applause.

During the time the audience is applauding, the performers must understand that they are receiving heartfelt gifts, and act accordingly. If the performers act like any of the first three co-workers in the Christmas story, the audience will watch the performance politely, applaud from time to time, and go home. They may enjoy the technical aspects of the performance; however, they won't get personally attached to the performer(s). If the performers respond like Stephanie, the audience will soon find gratification and inspiration. They will realize that the evening promises to be an enjoyable and mutually rewarding experience that consistently progresses from one level to the next. In the years that follow, the audience will remember that rewarding experience.

TYPES OF APPLAUSE

Now that you've have had a chance to look at how important applause is, it's time to drill down more deeply. As you will see, this chapter is devoted to applause and applause cycles. Applause is so important that it needs to be discussed thoroughly. We will cover four basic types of applause.

Courtesy or "Mercy" Applause – "Mercy" applause occurs when the audience is simply being polite. For the most part, this type of applause is disingenuous. An audience will always feel uncomfortable when they provide no response whatsoever, so they respond just enough to remain polite.

Warm, Constrained Applause – The audience wants to express their sincere appreciation, however they place a maximum threshold on it. The level of enthusiasm stays capped.

Hearty Applause – Hearty applause happens when individual audience members place their personal endorsement on the performance by clapping loudly. It's contagious.

Wild Applause – The audience goes crazy. A good example of wild applause is when the Beatles played at Shea Stadium in the 1960s. Police and doctors were on the scene hours before the show in order to assist the teenage girls, who were fainting by the hundreds.

READING APPLAUSE

It is of utmost importance that performers learn to continually and carefully listen to the applause, laughter and even silence from the audience in order to monitor the progress of the show. Once you are able to accurately measure the intensity and timing of audience responses, you can safely make decisions about how upcoming show elements should be paced. It is highly recommended that you not treat applause lightly or take it for granted.

Cultural Issues

In some countries around the world, audiences wait until the end of a show to applaud. This is a cultural practice and it is their way of being polite and respectful to the performer. Be careful to accurately interpret applause and an audience's response. I've known more than a few performers who have played in Japan for the first time, only to think that the audience's lack of response equaled disdain for the performer, when in reality their silence marked their respect and honor for the performer. Make yourself aware of local customs so that you can make correct assumptions with regard to the audience's response.

ACCEPTING APPLAUSE

For some performers, the time when the audience begins to applaud may be an opportunity to:

- Change a guitar string
- Get a drink of water
- Adjust the knobs on an amplifier
- Tell an inside joke to a fellow performer

It's not. In such a scenario, the gift of applause given by the audience and then ignored by the performer means the audience and their gift have no value. This, in effect, is a monumental snub on the part of the performer.

When a well-performed song has ended, it is time for the audience to respond. Applause is the audience's opportunity to show their appreciation to the performer. It is important that an audience be allowed every opportunity to show their appreciation by applauding, whistling, yelling, or otherwise. Applause is a gift that should always be openly received by all performers on the stage. **The art of accepting applause is one of the most valuable entertainment concepts to learn and cultivate.** It is the ultimate gesture a performer can use to demonstrate the value he or she places on the audience. It is an issue of worth and respect.

It is important that you not stop the applause prematurely by:

- Talking on the microphone over the applause and, thus, stifling it
- Turning your back to the audience
- Holding your arms out with your hands palms down, the universal signal to be quiet and stop applauding

- Telling an inside joke to a fellow performer
- Doing something that might be inconsiderate (as illustrated in the Christmas story)

How to Thank the Audience Without Causing Them to Stop Applauding

It is preferable for the audience to applaud as much as they would like to. The more the better! You don't want to stop them prematurely. However, you should thank them for their applause and you can do it while they are applauding. How do you accomplish this without killing the applause?

As soon as the applause begins:

- Step away from the microphone stand or, if you are using a handheld microphone, lower it to your side. This shows that you do not intend to start speaking over the sound system.
- Mouth the words "Thank You" and nod your head, with sincere appreciation, to individuals throughout the audience.
- At the point when applause begins to taper off, move back to the mic stand or lift the handheld mic and say "Thank You" audibly to advance to the next part of the show. This flow maintains pressure, continuity, and a proper pace.

THE PERFORMER'S LEVEL OF APPRECIATION

It is very important to note that you must measure the audience's level of enthusiasm and sincerity in order to know how best to respond. The intensity with which you respond should be commensurate with the intensity of the applause. If the audience expresses wild enthusiasm, you must match their enthusiasm level with your own enthusiastic "Thank Yous." If the applause is warm or hearty, you need to match it in like form.

In most cases, you will find that levels of enthusiasm and sincerity for a specific performing group are very similar from show to show and from town to town. You will find exceptions, however. This is where you must listen carefully and then be able to match the sincerity level as the situation dictates.

Funny Story about Loud Audiences

Quite a few years ago, I was hired to play with a multi-platinum band at the height of their career, the Backstreet Boys. We had done a few weeks of rehearsals and we were ready for our first show of the World Tour in Belgium. I had been fitted for in-ear monitors, but they weren't done yet. I wasn't terribly concerned, though, as I would have monitors on stage. Little did I realize that the in-ear monitors were not provided to merely monitor what myself and the band was to play. They were provided to protect me from the deafening screams coming from the thousands of young female fans in the audiences. I made it through the first concert – but I had my in-ear monitors in after that. I had never played in front of that many people, and I had never heard an audience scream like that before. I didn't know that was possible, and I was completely unprepared for the type of applause and how to handle it. Those 60,000 screaming fans taught me a great lesson. Applause styles and cycles differ with each performance situation. Once I dealt with bringing down the sheer volume of the love being shown to us, I could enjoy it, accept it and revel in it.

APPLAUSE CYCLES

An applause cycle is the response curve that explains the timing of changes in the intensity level of an audience's applause.

Applause Cycles Are Not All Created Equal

Each audience has a slightly different applause cycle. Some start and build more quickly than others. Some retain their peak level longer. Some taper off more quickly than others. Because of this, it is imperative that you sense the timing of an audience's applause cycle very early in the show so you can correctly adjust the timing of transitions throughout the remainder of the show.

Normal Applause Cycle

Applause starts from nothing and quickly grows to a peak. Once it has maintained its peak for a period of time, it gradually descends. It is this basic applause cycle that will serve as your time-pacing tool for the entire show.

Figure 9 below shows a normal applause cycle that rises to a peak fairly quickly, remains there for a short amount of time and then starts to gradually diminish.

Normal Applause Cycle

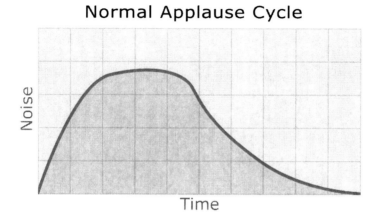

Figure 9: Normal Applause Cycle

Using the Applause Cycle as a Time Cue

Please view Figure 10 below. At which of the four numbered points do you think the ideal time would be to start the next song?

1. As the applause is getting louder?
2. During the peak level of the applause?
3. When the applause begins to subside?
4. After the applause has died down completely?

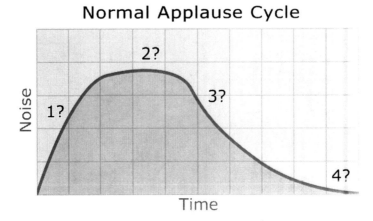

Figure 10: When to start the next song?

Below are related comments and the answer:

1. If you start the next song as the applause is getting louder, you will be prematurely telling the audience to quiet
down. This will convey to the audience that you feel their
participation is not important. They will stop applauding
because they have been instructed to do so.
2. If you start the next song when the applause is at its peak,
you face two risks as follows:
   (A) You may not fully understand the audience's intent as
   demonstrated by their applause. They may be
   preparing themselves to clap even louder!
   (B) The audience may wish to <u>continue</u> clapping at this
   peak level in order to demonstrate their appreciation.
   Either way, you risk telling them to quiet down
   prematurely.
3. **Question mark 3 is correct.** It's best to start the next song
at the point where the applause has started to wind down.
You maintain momentum and you have allowed the audience time to respond.

4. Do not wait to start the next song until the applause has died down completely, because there will have been a period of no direction. You will have let all of the air out of the balloon and will be left with "dead air."

Figure 11 below describes the ideal place to start the next song or event. It also points out the area that is typically referred to as "dead air."

Normal Applause Cycle

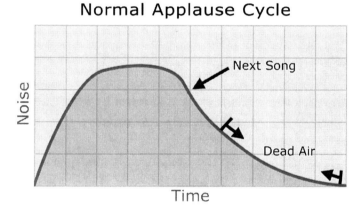

Figure 11: Proper Time For Next Song

Song Endings Trigger and Influence Applause Cycles

Usually, it is the **ending** of a particular event (song, joke, etc.) that triggers applause. With live music, two main types of endings are common. One of the most dramatic endings is sometimes referred to as a "Trashcan Ending." This is where the musicians hit the last big chord and continually sustain it at a fever pitch with the drummer crashing drums and cymbals. This is the last big chord that no other chord could follow thereby leaving no doubt in the audience's mind that this is definitely the end.

The other type of ending is trickier. It's typically a surprise/shock ending. This is where the song ends sharply before the audience is prepared. Once the audience notices that the song is over, a few seconds later, they typically clap according to their enthusiasm level at the moment.

It is recommended that different types of endings be used for the sake of variety during the course of a show since this tends to make the show more interesting. At the same time, it's good to place the surprise endings in places only after you have built a solid relationship with the audience.

Complex Applause Cycles

Double Applause Cycle

A Double Applause Cycle is created as a result of the interaction of two show events that take place concurrently. For example, a Double Applause Cycle can occur when a "signature song" (instantly recognizable by the audience) begins just after the peak of the previous song's applause cycle. The audience will tend to clap louder as soon as the highly recognizable song starts. This scenario is illustrated below in Figure 12. Another way to achieve a Double Applause Cycle could be to start a different song at the end of an individual solo or event while the audience is still applauding.

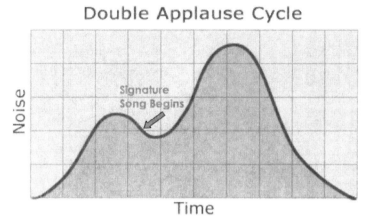

Figure 12: Double Applause Cycle

Triple Applause Cycle

A Triple Applause Cycle can be an extraordinary event. One scenario that might achieve a Triple Applause Cycle is as follows: At the ending of a song, the audience claps (normal applause cycle). The performers, at the proper point in the applause cycle, begin their signature song (double applause cycle). All of a sudden a superstar makes a surprise appearance just after the signature song begins taking the enthusiasm level to still greater heights. This scenario is illustrated in Figure 13 below:

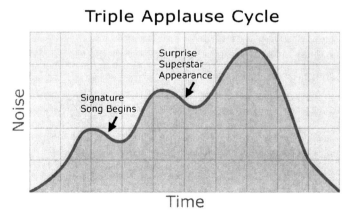

Figure 13: Triple Applause Cycle

Applause cycles are the by-products of a well-designed show flow. The process of performing in a show with great content selection, excellent pacing, and the proper handling of applause cycles can maintain a high degree of intensity throughout a show. If you can achieve this, you'll find people talking about the show for weeks afterward to their friends. They may even say it's the best show they've ever seen.

Timing Is Everything!
The amount of time that applause cycles take to ramp up, stay at the top, and finally decline varies from audience to audience and room to room. Because of this, is it important to carefully listen to the applause, early in the show, so that you can calibrate your pacing for the remainder of the performance. The phrase "listen to the applause" may sound a bit odd since many might wonder how a performer could avoid hearing it. The point to remember is as follows:

Performers are often filled with nervous enthusiasm when performing in front of a crowd. They become so absorbed with their immediate concerns such as what is the next song, which guitar will they be playing, etc. that they don't pay enough attention to other important show details such as applause. Learn to carefully listen to applause. Monitoring, understanding, and reacting successfully to applause can be a key factor to your success. It enables you to properly evaluate the audience's current level of enthusiasm and use this information to make slight adjustments necessary to take things up to the next level.

HOW ACOUSTICS AFFECT APPLAUSE CYCLES

Indoors: The acoustics at an entertainment venue can affect an audience's response. For instance, rooms with live acoustics (hard, reflective surfaces) tend to quickly amplify and retain the sound of applause. This tends to cause an audience to accelerate and intensify their response. The more applause they hear, the more they feel like applauding.

Outdoors: The lack of acoustic reflective surfaces outdoors tends to cause applause or laughter to die down quickly and unexpectedly. Because of this, the applause cycle at an outdoor venue can be much shorter as you will see in Figure 13 below. There are two things for the performer to keep in mind:

1. Do your best to obtain the highest degree of enthusiasm from an outdoor audience. This may help to counterbalance the lack of acoustic reflection.

2. Condition yourself to realize that outdoor environments are different, however, the audience is still enjoying the show. Learn to adjust to the acoustic differences between indoor and outdoor venues and make the most of them.

Figure 14 below compares an outdoor applause cycle with that of a normal one:

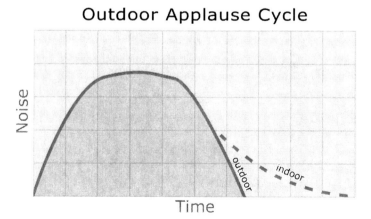

Figure 14: Outdoor Applause Cycle

END OF THE SHOW APPLAUSE TIPS

The audience must be informed when the show is coming to an end. There are many reasons for this. The audience may be so happy with the performance that they may wish to fully express their gratitude when the show finally comes to an end. These potential expressions of gratitude may need a bit of time to prepare mentally. Audience members may have "after-show" logistical concerns that need attention such as locating a friend, taking pictures, gathering belongings, and other things that will help them prepare for the upcoming, and hopefully senti-mental, "good-bye."

You will find that the proper signaling of the show ending will yield good rewards. For one, you will find an audience that is fully prepared to express their gratitude at the highest levels they will allow themselves.

On the other hand, a surprise show ending could leave an audience feeling a bit confused and disoriented. They may even feel disappointed, and possibly ripped off. When this happens, the performers might hear a few "boos!" The best way for performers to protect themselves against such a negative reaction is to let the audience know, in some way, that the show will soon be coming to an end. This can be accomplished in a number of ways.

1. Dedicate the final song to an important person or a group of people.
2. Inform the audience how much of a pleasure it's been to play for them.
3. Express regret that the show must soon come to an end with this last song.

You can achieve the optimum end-of-show reaction from the audience by pre-announcing the last song and then providing a larger-than-life ending to the song by employing a "trashcan" ending. Any number of creative endings can be devised for the show; however, it is important that the proper signals be sent to the audience, or confusion may be introduced at this critical point in time.

THE STANDING OVATION

Think back when you attended a show of one of your favorite recording artists. The show was so "off the charts" sensational that the audience leapt to their feet, in a standing ovation, after the last song was played. Remember how special and satisfied it felt to be a part of that outpouring of affection that was being showered onto the artist? A standing ovation can be just as memorable an experience for the audience members as it is for the artist.

When you have performed in front of enough audiences, you'll end up experiencing virtually every situation imaginable. You will experience a great audience that will give you standing ovations after almost every song, even when the show is less than your best. You will also find very difficult audiences that will barely clap, even when the show is excellent. When it comes to standing ovations, though, they're typically hard to come by. As each member of the audience must individually decide whether he or she will "endorse" the performance, there are a number of forces and dynamics that come into play that are often beyond the control of the performers. The results can be exhilarating or they can be humbling.

Standing ovations are <u>earned</u> by the combination of a well-paced outstanding performance and the close bond that has been forged between the performer and individual members of the audience. This bond is important since audience members will be more prone to give a standing ovation to someone they feel is a valued friend. The individual audience members decide whether or not to give a standing ovation based upon how they feel.

The "Not Quite Sure" Standing Ovation

The "Not Quite Sure" experience and thought process may be something like this:

The show is over and the audience starts to clap. A few people here and there stand up and clap heartily. An audience member thinks, "Hmm... Should I stand up?" He or she also wonders, "What if I'm one of the first to stand up? Will I look foolish? Maybe I'll stand up if a few more people do." They eventually stand up and start to clap heartily as well. He or she admits, "Okay, they got me. They won me over. They now have my personal endorsement." Soon enough they're happy that they stood up and made a statement, and they're also happy that the people around them seem to have come to the same conclusion.

Note: As you can see, the people around you can influence your decision to participate in the standing ovation. If the people around you are not inclined to stand up, you will most likely not stand up either. If the people around you jump to their feet, you will most likely think about providing your own valuable endorsement and then stand up, if you agree that it has been earned. The important thing for the performer to note is that the standing ovation is most likely not the result of excellent technical execution. It is almost always the result of having developed a great relationship with the audience, in addition to a solid performance. If this relationship has not been built properly, a standing ovation is not a guaranteed result.

The "Leaping" Ovation

Sometimes the show is so overwhelming, in all aspects, that the audience is primed and ready to explode with gratitude after the last song. As soon as they recognize the show has reached its end, the audience will enthusiastically jump to their feet in order to register their hearty approval of the performers as well as the performance itself. The greater the show, the easier the decision is for the audience to stand up.

Ways to Encourage the Audience to Stand Up

A standing ovation occurs when the audience overflows with emotion and gratitude for what it has just experienced. This can be due to a more impressive than usual solo, a magical performance of one of their favorite songs, a heartfelt moment that was shared, or simply as the culmination of a spectacularly executed show. The pressure and magic have built up inside the audience to the point where they are prepared to make an emphatic statement. In some cases, however, they aren't quite sure how (or when) to make their statement. In these cases, the audience may need a little direction. Here are a few steps to try the next time you're working towards your standing ovation.

1. When the audience starts to applaud, thank the audience off the microphone with arms outstretched and your palms facing upward.
2. Do your best to look everyone in the audience in the eye as you're expressing your gratitude.

3. Don't feel rushed to get off the stage or talk to the audience over the microphone. Talking over applause cuts off the applause because the audience wants to hear what you're saying, so they stop clapping in order to hear you. Let them clap as long as the applause maintains it's peak level.
4. While acknowledging the applause, look at the other performers as if to say, "Aren't these people great?"
5. Take one or two steps forward. This will help to increase the pressure on the audience to give even more of themselves. Do not step backward since this will release pressure.
6. Express more sincere gratitude off-mic directly toward the audience.
7. Exercise a bit of patience while the clapping continues.
8. Look to a few people standing in the audience, as if you know them personally, and express your gratitude or make a friendly hand gesture toward them. Give them a visual "Thank You." Other members of the audience will see this and want to be included. This personal interaction reminds the audience of the bond that has been created between you.
9. Be sure to show that you are emotionally overwhelmed by their generous response. Remind yourself of the incredible bond you've made with this audience and show them how you feel. This tends to make them want to respond even more.
10. In the end, it is important to leave the audience wanting more. Leave while the audience is still at its peak of applause.

If the audience has no intention of standing up, they won't and it's probably best to say a few kind words, thank the audience and call it a night. You'll get them to stand up for you the next time!

THE ENCORE

Now you've achieved your standing ovation. You've played an amazing show, made a real connection that you and the audience values, accepted their applause with grace, and now you're listening to the roar of the audience from off stage. They won't leave until you return to play them another song. This is the ultimate seal of approval from an audience. So how do you make the most of this?

There are a few ways to go when choosing a correct song for an encore.

1. After the standing ovation, you have the audience in the palm of your hand. You've created a frenzy of excitement and intensity. Keep it going with one of their favorite up-tempo songs that maintains this excitement and celebratory level, and builds it even more. Show the audience you can even take them farther than what drove them to a standing ovation in the first place.

2. You have the audience in the palm of your hand. You've won over the audience and have received a standing ovation. Now they want more and you can choose to show them a different side of you. Play an acoustic song with just you. Sing or play a song that will draw on people's emotions and or feelings differently than the "hit you over the head" approach you took to end the show. Surprise is always a great element to use to your benefit, but only use this option if you feel certain you can captivate them with just you or a very sparse arrangement. It's very important to not let the pressure release, but to change its course a bit. Then, follow this song with one of their favorite up-tempo songs to leave on a high, celebratory note.

CHAPTER EIGHT

DO'S AND DON'TS

Sometimes all you want is a simple list of Do's and Don'ts. As you will see, these do's and don'ts fit into the overall concepts of a good show as presented above.

DO MAKE A GREAT FIRST IMPRESSION

- First impressions are lasting impressions.
- Know who you are as an artist, and commit to that 100%.
- Have a definable "look."
- Greet the audience confidently and treat them as your friend. Be at ease with the audience.

DO PAY TRIBUTE TO THE AUDIENCE

- Take the audience on a rewarding journey.
- Compliment the audience throughout the show. "You people are great! What a great audience! We're enjoying playing for you!"
- Maintain show pressure.
- Prevent dead air.
- Create a bond with the audience through one-to-one communication skills.
- Employ proper acceptance of applause, which creates even more applause.
- Take the show to a successful and fulfilling conclusion.

DO EXHIBIT HONESTY AND SINCERITY
TO AN AUDIENCE

A high quality performance must exude honesty and sincerity. Audiences can detect when a performer is not being genuine. As a champion poker player can identify subtle tendencies in an opponent, so audiences can likewise identify subtle movements and expressions in a performer that may help them to spot a phony. The best strategy is to live a genuine life and allow the transparency of your performance to signal that you're who you say you are, and your music is truly reflective of that.

DO COMPLIMENT YOUR AUDIENCE

Have you ever attended a concert when the artist complimented the audience with grace and style? Do you remember how it made you feel? It's this feeling that you want to replicate in the hearts of your audiences. You do this by sincerely paying them compliments and by thanking them appropriately. They didn't have to show up for the show. They didn't have to applaud and show their appreciation as they did. The artist should be vulnerable and sensitive enough to feel honest appreciation and, in turn, to respond in a like manner to the audience.

One of the best times to begin complimenting the audience is following the opening song or group of songs. As the music stops and the audience's applause begins to die down, humbly tell the audience, "Wow, you people are great!" You might even look around to other band members and point to the audience as if to say, "Aren't they a great audience!" When the audience sees and hears this, they immediately feel appreciated and move into a more intimate feeling of involvement with your show. It is amazing that many bands and performers ignore this most basic bit of performance etiquette.

If you sincerely compliment your audience throughout the show, the relationship and bond will be strengthened even further. You will become more than just a performer. You will become their friend.

DO SAY THE RIGHT THINGS

The 100% Rule: Do and Say Things That Work 100% of the Time

Obviously it's best to be extemporaneous if you're able. This is an enormous advantage for those who have a quick wit. If you don't have such a quick wit, you can get along by saying the same things night after night… *as long as you say the right things.*

Few people realize that some of the greatest entertainers of all time say the same things, in the same way, at every show. Over time, they have found the rhythm that works for them and this rhythm takes the audience on the prescribed journey. Once they find something that consistently works, they cling to it and use it every night and speak the words as if it were the first time they've ever said them. This last part is very important, since saying the same things every night can become boring to you as the performer. What keeps it from becoming boring is taking on the challenge of selling it to each audience as something new and spontaneous, and getting the desired response from them night after night. Realize that the audience is hearing this for the first time, so you must present it as "fresh" every night. This can be work!

Every once in a while a great entertainer might allow him or herself the luxury of trying something new. If it works, they may try it again (just to see if it's a fluke). Once they establish it as being <u>bulletproof,</u> they leave it in the act. If the percentages don't work to their satisfaction, they typically throw it out.

The 100% rule also applies to your artistic performance. When you find that something you play results in a very positive response from the audience every time, it is a good idea to use it regularly. Consistency is a very good thing when the routine works every time.

100% Rule Story #1
A well-known singing star was playing to an enthusiastic crowd in a Las Vegas showroom. Somewhere around the middle of the show he stopped everything and, in a very casual and personal manner, complimented the audience and told them that "It isn't normal practice to do this, but the orchestra and I have been working up a really great new song for our show and what better place to rehearse it than in front of friends like you" (and he gestured out into the audience). The audience was immediately touched by such a personalized remark and began to applaud. At that point he and the orchestra performed the song flawlessly to a very enraptured audience. This seemingly off-the-cuff gesture created a major impact on the audience. They felt special to have shared in such a monumental moment with the performer. What they didn't know was that during his show on the following night, he stopped the show at the same point, and said and did exactly the same thing. That "new" song was the same every night. He ended up giving every audience this very special moment and doing it in a way that came across as if it were the first and only time he had done it.

100% Rule Story #2

After playing a very popular and well-known guitar solo the same way night after night for adoring fans, John decided he was not being true to his "artistic self." He felt that his creativity was being stifled by the constant repetition. As a result, John decided to just improvise his solo, not for the purpose of improving the show, but to demonstrate his abilities as a guitarist and improvisor. The fans tolerated the changes made to John's signature solo; however, there was never the same response to the improvised solos as there was to the well-known signature solo. Likewise, the other band members were a bit confused and thrown off guard, as they could not support John in his new solo like they had done previously. They weren't sure what he was doing or where he was going. In the end, an influential band member approached John and mentioned the improvisation was appreciated on an artistic level, but the show had lost some of its sizzle because of it. An important opportunity in the show was lost and this band member wanted to know if there was a way to reinstate the solo as it was before. In the end, John abandoned the improvisation and returned to the popular, signature solo. In the process, John noticed the difference in the responses from the audience and learned a valuable lesson. He realized that the integrity and continuity of the show was more important to the audience than he had originally suspected. One reason for this is that fans develop affection for solos, and when they are deprived of hearing each nuance of that loved solo they can feel disappointed.

DON'T EVER TURN YOUR BACK TO THE AUDIENCE

It's generally a bad idea to turn your back on the audience unless you are performing a deliberate movement or routine. By simply turning your back on an audience for no apparent reason, a number of non-verbal messages are sent as follows:

- You're not important
- I'm more important than you
- I'm so caught up in me that I've forgotten you
- This show is not all that important

As you can imagine, pressure is being released by these non-verbal messages allowing an audience to focus its attention on other things and other thoughts. By maintaining eye contact with the audience and doing your best to "work the crowd," you should be able to sustain an acceptable level of pressure for retaining the crowd's attention and participation. This is hard to do when your back is turned.

DON'T REFER TO THE AUDIENCE (DIRECTLY) AS FANS

It is recommended that you not refer to the audience as "fans" when you are speaking to them directly. This is a little presumptive and impersonal. Although it is certainly not the worst thing you can say, it's much better to use words such as:

- You guys
- All
- Everyone who's been so supportive
- Friends
- You good people

DO ENDEAR YOURSELF TO AN AUDIENCE

The audience wants to make a connection with you. They want to feel like you're one of them. Create a bond any way you can.

- Relate to a common bond between the audience members. Different cities and different environments call for different approaches. Are you playing to a crowd of contest winners from a radio station? Hello, winners! Are you playing in Texas? Texans are very proud of their state. If you draw attention to the fact that you're in Texas, such as greeting the audience by saying "Hello, Texas!" or "I'm so glad to be in Texas!" - you win.
- Do you have family in the town you're playing? Make the audience aware of that connection. It makes them feel that you're more a part of their world.
- Do you know any current sports scores or general feelings about the local teams? Share them. It lets people know you're in tune with the community, and that you truly care about what they care about.
- Have you played this town before? Mention that!
- Did you have a great burger in town earlier today? References made to various local establishments tend to further ingratiate the entertainers with the audience. For instance by saying, "When we first got into town we, of course, had to get a hamburger at Fred's Burger Joint." A well-placed reference such as this can elicit applause and endear the performers to the audience with relatively little effort.
- Make the audience feel like you're speaking to them as friends. True vulnerability is endearing. Open yourself up to them. Allow them to feel that they're taking a piece of you with them when they leave.

DON'T FORGET WHERE YOU ARE

Seriously. One error that occurs from time-to-time is you may forget where you are. You may say, "It's great to be here in New York" when you are in Boston. This is where it is important to be mentally prepared and do your homework before the show. This may seem trivial and even nonsensical to someone new to the road, but anyone with experience would definitely say that constant travel will eventually wear you down and make you have "brain freezes" at inopportune times. An easy fix is to make sure the name of the city or region you are performing in that particular night is written somewhere on the stage. This same rule applies to thanking sponsors or the local radio station. If you have to write it down and have it by you on stage, then do it. Mistakes like this are very hard to recover from. Prepare a bit, and you'll do great!

DO TRY TO ADD AUDIENCE PARTICIPATION

Whenever possible, create situations in the show that involve the audience playing a part.

- A bit of comedy where the audience can laugh out loud
- Call and response (Everybody scream!)
- Question and answer (band asks questions and audience answers)
- Sing-alongs
- Clap-alongs
- Bring people up onto the stage for a carefully choreographed routine
- Go out, into the audience, and have fun with the fans

This is typically successful because members of the audience immediately involve themselves at a much deeper level. In addition, the audience will always empathize with the unlucky individual(s) selected by the performers, or wish it were them with whom you were interacting. Either way, you win!

The best example I can think of is Bruce Springsteen in concert pulling an unknown Courtney Cox onstage to dance with him as every other girl was freaking out wishing it were her.

DO WATCH AND PROTECT THE SHOW TIMING

Make sure the various events within the show flow properly and effectively. Try your best to analyze the applause cycles and the feel of the intensity of the audience so you can effectively adjust and/or be aware of the correct flow of the show. You have ultimate control over which songs you play when, and how you interact with the audience in between. You want to make sure you are not missing opportunities to be more entertaining.

DON'T CATCH THE AUDIENCE OFF GUARD

When you're trying to involve the audience in some way, possibly with an audience participation sequence, it is important that you don't take them by surprise. If you ask for their involvement too early, or if they don't understand exactly what you want, they may just sit there and stare back at you. They may even appear to be uncooperative. In a worst case, it could become very embarrassing. An example of improper timing creating a negative impact on a show is as follows:

A very talented band was performing in a popular nightclub. Everything was going well until the band decided to engage in audience participation in the form of a sing-along. Unfortunately, nobody had prepared the audience beforehand. When it came time for this sing-along to start, the lead singer quickly pointed the microphone in the direction of the audience and waited for a response. You can probably tell what happened - nothing. The call to action was too abrupt and the audience didn't understand what was expected of them. The lead singer had to do a lot of extra work in order to recover.

It's far better to tell the audience what you want them to do. You may even want to have them practice a few times so there is no confusion. In many cases, audiences enjoy this type of inter-action. The involvement tends to break the monotony (if any) and, provides a platform for the audience to express themselves.

When you ask the audience to participate and they don't, it counts as a LOSS for the performers. NEVER ask an audience to do something unless you are sure they are ready, willing, and able to do it. Additionally, audience participation should never be scheduled toward the beginning of a show. You should wait until a strong rapport and a certain level of trust develops between the performer(s) and the audience.

DON'T SHOW YOURSELF BEFORE
THE SHOW STARTS

Analogy: The groom shouldn't see the bride before the wedding.

It's always a good idea to not allow the audience to see you before you go on stage. Don't ruin the Disney magic. Being invisible until the show starts gives you an "edge" by providing you with the opportunity to make a greater first impression with your clothes, your attitude, your talent, etc. If people see you before a show, you may lose a bit of your edge, especially if you look like an ordinary person on the street. Such a sighting may dissolve some of you and/or your band's mystique.

The "mystique" issue relates to an unconscious grasp of "behavioral economics" – supply and demand. If a performer is "supplied" or available with the houselights on in ordinary street clothes, etc., he/she is immediately viewed as less desirable, at least unconsciously. Keep your mystique and surprise them when you walk on stage.

DON'T SHIELD YOUR EYES FROM THE LIGHTS

Don't let the audience know the lights are blinding you. One common mistake is to try to shield your eyes from the lights while looking out into the audience. This tells the audience that you cannot see them and it will tip them off that your attempts to communicate (one-to-one) are disingenuous.

DO STAND DIRECTLY IN THE LIGHTS

This is a very important point that is constantly overlooked by performers. The lights are there to make you shine and to make you look good. You are the performer, and you need to be seen by the audience. Use the lights to your advantage, as a film director would use them to bring out certain shots and certain scenes. Are you playing a featured solo? Get right into the brightest light on stage. Stand in it. Bask in it. Don't move over to the side of the stage out of the lights where you are difficult to see. "In the lights" is where the show is happening. As you're gaining expertise with using light to your advantage, you'll learn to move in and out of different colors of lights and different intensities of lights to make points in your show more powerful. Are you singing about something sad or poignant? Use the colored lights to make the feel moodier. Are you making a point and need to be seen? Make sure you're right in the brightest light. It works! If you are blinded by the lights, you are standing in the right place.

DO USE TRASHCAN ENDINGS AT THE END OF THE SHOW

The end of the show is a crucial time that cannot be underestimated. It's the time when the performers will ask the audience to make a final decision regarding their efforts for the night. This is no time to surprise the audience with an unexpected ending. Not only should the ending be nice and long, its length and intensity should be unique. This final ending should be a signal to the audience that the show is clearly over. This will give the audience plenty of time to decide how best to orient themselves so they can respond appropriately. A "trashcan" ending is an ending that holds out the last note for a length of time appropriate to build intensity. With every strum of the guitar and every fill the drummer plays, the audience becomes more and more frantic as they anxiously await their chance to show their appreciation for a great show. This is your final build up of pressure to then release and let the audience go wild.

DO ASSUME THE AUDIENCE HAS NEVER SEEN THE SHOW BEFORE

Some performers become paranoid that too many people have already seen the show and they change it unnecessarily. In some cases, this may be a legitimate concern. In most cases, it's best to assume that the vast majority has never seen the show. If something works night to night, don't be afraid to use it. Remember the 100% Rule. You can feel comfortable performing the same show in exactly the same way with no fear knowing that everything will run smoothly. In the cases where people really have seen the show, they actually enjoy seeing the same thing over again (note for note and word for word.) They love to demonstrate their knowledge of the show to the people around them. This makes them feel like an insider. In other cases, people are equally entertained, as they may not clearly remember the details of the show anyway.

DO HAVE A LOT OF FUN ON STAGE

Perhaps you have heard someone tell you that you need to LOOK more like you're having fun. Maybe you are having fun, but you don't portray it well to your audience. This makes a big difference in winning an audience over. People want to see you enjoying yourself. Think of how you look from the audience's perspective, not your own. You may be having a blast, but be standing motionless onstage looking bored. How do you look like you're having fun? There are a few ways.

1. Smile. Be aware of yourself on stage. Move with the music. Show your emotion. If all you can muster is a smile, that's all right. Build up to movement on stage.

Build up to making the audience more a part of your emotion and performance. A smile goes a long way!

2. Make it real! Have so much fun on stage that you can't contain yourself. Then you don't have to pretend. It's real. The hope is that it is infectious and spills out into the audience. Consider the alternatives: A 9 to 5 job? Corporate life? Flipping burgers? In other words, play!

3. A great way to learn if you look like you're having fun on stage is to video yourself. You may think you know what you look like when you're performing. You never look quite like what you think you do. Study your movements and your facial expressions. Are you communicating to the audience? Are you conveying how much fun you're having? Are you conveying the passion that you feel when you play or sing? If not, work towards opening up that part of you and sharing it with the audience. It'll pay off!

A Quick Story

A very prominent jazz guitarist, Peter White, always loved being on stage. It was where he felt the most comfortable pouring out his heart through his guitar to the audience. The only problem was, the audience couldn't tell that he was enraptured. He just stood there and closed his eyes on stage and played. He always felt as if his feelings were conveyed until he saw a performance coach who told him otherwise. The coach told him that he looked miserable while he was playing. And it wasn't until Peter saw himself playing that he realized the coach was right. He did look miserable. But that was the furthest thing from his mind as he was playing. He had to tap into the feelings of joy he was feeling and make sure that the audience was feeling the same thing. It took a bit of soul searching, but today Peter White is an absolutely captivating performer. He conveys every bit of joy he feels every night to every member of the audience.

DO WORK HARD ON STAGE

Work so hard on stage that you don't think you can make it through the show. A possible barometer may be to ensure that you are dripping with sweat by the second song in the show. Entertainers who work very hard on stage have historically had a stronger impact on audiences. James Brown had the reputation of being "The Hardest Working Man in Show Business." People like to see you sweat because they know you're exerting effort and energy for their benefit. They feel they are getting their money's worth.

Note: This may not work with every performer's identity. Some performers such as Josh Groban may be able to sing and emote everything he needs to in order to win the audience over, while the members of Linkin Park need to really show intensity and physical effort.

DO THANK THE PEOPLE WHO BROUGHT YOU HERE

You have a unique power as a performer to thank the important people to your career from the stage and therefore win some brownie points. Did the local radio station come down and support you? Are they playing your music? Thank them. Not only will it endear you to your audience, it'll make the radio station know that you appreciate them and their support. They'll want to support you more in the future because of this show of gratitude.

Also thank the promoter of the show. If you're playing a club, thank the club owner or booker. They stuck their neck out and took a chance on you. Are you playing a theater or festival?

Thank the promoter for putting on such a great show. You and the audience can bond over what a great night you're having.

Are you taking the stage following another artist's set? If so, compliment them too.

Is someone like Budweiser or Lexus sponsoring your tour? Thank them. Say something great about their product. Being kind publicly to the people who helped you get in front of this audience is invaluable, and will help you build a rapport with those people and build a relationship for future performances.

DO YOUR BEST TO SHOW COURTESY AND RESPECT

Common Courtesy: When someone opens for you they must wait while you do your sound check before they can do theirs. Some headliners have misused this perk. They tend to goof-off during the sound check causing it to run overtime and impinge on the opening act's sound check time. This, as a result, causes the opening act to get a less than adequate sound check.

It's a professional courtesy to go through your sound check in a deliberate and timely manner so as not to short-change the opening act. It reflects poorly on the headliner when they allow themselves a lot of time to goof-off at the detriment of the lesser-known opening act. Remember, "Be careful how you treat people on the way up the ladder because you could very well meet them again on the way down."

ALWAYS treat your technical crew with the utmost of respect. These are people behind the scenes working hard to ensure that everything goes smoothly for you. Often, they go without sleep to do this and handle multiple jobs simultaneously. For example, it's not uncommon to find out that the guy at the mixer board also drives the 18-wheeler (truck). They stand in the shadows, out of the limelight. Most of them have an exemplary attitude of service that causes them to give of themselves.

Show your appreciation as often as you can. Let them know you recognize the importance and value of what they do. This will go a long way. You need these people on your side.

DON'T TREAT A RETURN ENGAGEMENT LIGHTLY

When an artist returns to the same town and plays another engagement it usually happens because the prior engagement was successful. The promoter did well enough the first time around and, after seeing the positive response from the audience, decides to bring the artist back again. There are two important elements here:

- The promoter
- The fans

A promoter chooses an act that he/she feels will have sufficient drawing power to sell enough tickets to pay the bills and hopefully turn a profit. Furthermore, such a promoter is gratified when the fans are pleased with the show and demonstrate their desire to see more (great) shows in the future. The entire event is a gamble on the promoter's part. Any number of factors could cause a show to fail. There could be a blizzard, the local college team could end up in the finals, or a hurricane could come through the area a month prior and destroy the venue. The one factor that provides some level of comfort to the promoter is the performer's ability to attract and then please the audience.

Let's say that, on the night of the concert, the weather was perfect, the venue was packed, the sound system was great and the artist got three standing ovations. The promoter will be very inclined to bring the performer back for a return engagement.

It is important that the artist realizes that this return engagement is the result of a valuable bond that was formed at the prior show, maybe as much as a year ago. Many new fans were made and word of mouth spread about the highly successful concert. By the time the return engagement comes around, all of the people with tickets will experience eager anticipation. By the time the lights come on onstage, the audience will be ready for a major love-fest.

It is imperative that the artist display warmth, affection and a great deal of appreciation for the fact that so many people paid their hard-earned money and showed up again. After the applause following the opening sequence has begun to subside, the artist needs to welcome everyone to the show and tell the audience how pleased he/she is to be back here in <u>name of the city</u> and be able to play for this audience once again that now seems to be populated by old friends. It needs to be said as if it is the first time you've ever said it and it needs to be sincere. If you think about it, you would be extremely fortunate to have a loyal following anywhere and tonight you have one sitting right in front of you. The audience will sense your sincerity and your love-fest will begin.

DO ACT AS IF YOU <u>TRULY</u> LIKE THE OTHER PERFORMERS ON STAGE

This is essential! As you begin to spend time with band mates (or other colleagues you share a stage with), you will find that you can't like everyone. People tend to get on other people's nerves for numerous reasons. (Certainly more reasons than can be identified in this book.) It is therefore quite likely that, when the show starts, one or more of the performers will be harboring some type of grudge against one another.

The audience will actually look at the performers for cues about how to feel about the performers on stage. It's best to model the attitudes you'd like the audience to have toward everyone else on stage.

What to do: It's important that all of the behind-the-scenes dramas be suspended once the curtain goes up. I was in a band that backstage would be cursing each other continually and sometimes come to blows before taking the stage. When the show started, though, they looked like best friends. Performers must act as if they respect, admire, and enjoy each other's presence on stage. In fact, everyone should act as if they've never had so much fun (playing in such a great place)…together. Once the show is over, the performers can go back to hating each other if they so choose.

DON'T SPEAK POORLY OF ANOTHER ARTIST

Never "knock" another artist. It will reflect poorly upon you and could very well come back to bite you some day. Negativity in any form onstage is useless and usually ends up hurting the show in some way. Rule of Thumb: If you can't say anything nice about someone, don't say anything at all. People who try to blow out someone else's candle to make theirs shine brighter end up looking dimmer. And people you meet on the way up you may very well meet on the way down.

CHAPTER NINE

SOLOING

A SOLO OCCURS WHEN AN INDIVIDUAL ON
STAGE HAS THE OPPORTUNITY TO SHARE A
PERSONAL AND/OR IMPROVISED MUSICAL
JOURNEY WITH THE AUDIENCE.

The types of solos being referred to here are when instrumentalists take the spotlight by demonstrating brilliant technical skills. A well-executed solo is one of the few "slam-dunk" opportunities to get the audience on your side. If the solo is well executed and leads to a dramatic climax, there is no reason why an audience wouldn't become involved.

Please bear in mind that the majority of audience members are not master musicians, so the following solo recommendations will take this fact into account.

The purpose of solo playing is to give an individual performer the opportunity to create a unique musical experience for the audience through the art of improvisation. Historically, there has always been the issue of "who are we trying to impress?" It seems that some musicians are mainly trying to impress the musicians in the audience with their musical prowess. Sadly, this practice can leave the less musically savvy members of the audience feeling left out when the player reaches a technical or artistic level that is over their heads. The challenge is to improvise in such a way that the audience can become involved and remain involved in the solo to the benefit of everyone. Play to your audience, not above them. A more musically sophisticated traditional jazz audience will expect a different solo than a pop audience. The pop audience will want to hear the solo from the record that they know and love, and the jazz audience will want to be moved by the technical brilliance of the performer.

Think of a solo in the same way as you do a complete show. There should be an opener, hills and valleys, and a closer (big ending). As the music transitions into the beginning of the solo, you must first gain the attention of the audience and establish that you are now going to become the focal point. If you are able to move around on stage, you should position yourself at the front of the stage. Begin the solo by playing something that is relatively simple and musically infectious. Once you have their attention, you can now carefully lead them along by improvising music that they are able to grasp. Take them on a journey.

Speaking of gaining an audience's attention and becoming the focal point, on tour one summer, my band members each came up with a signature to get the audience to know it was time for their solo. It started by accident one night when the bass player stopped playing to push up his sleeves because it was 105 degrees, and the audience, surprisingly, started cheering. We all took note of that and talked about experimenting with ways we could get the audience to prepare for and focus on each of our solos. Every night the bass player stopped playing abruptly and pushed up his sleeves at the top of his solo. It worked every time. My guitarist played one note and just let it ring and feed-back. He'd stand while his guitar just whined and distorted on this one note, and he'd drink a bottle of water. People loved it. My drummer would stand up and take off his watch and hand it to me. The crowd would go wild. What a lesson we all learned that summer…some of the simplest things can set the stage for a great solo and a lot of audience focus on you.

I've seen some great solos in my time, but some of the best in my opinion involve some sort of performance value. I played with a drummer who would slowly build his solo from a few sparing hits to a barrage of cymbals and double bass drum flourishes. He usually ended his solo doing the dance move "running man" while still wowing you with his solo. This brought the house down. People were on their feet. Although he was surrounded by great players in the band who played more technically proficient solos, none of them got a standing ovation like he did. I'm not saying to dumb down, but I do recommend you knowing your audience. He knew his audience!

When contemplating a solo strategy there are several points to consider:

1. The Setting (Venue size, indoors/outdoors, big festival/ small intimate club)

Question: Is the setting one at which the performance is focused more on critical musical listening than on entertainment? Or, is it a festival where everyone is there to "party" and enjoy being part of an "event"? For instance, at some outdoor festivals the audience sits on blankets, eats and drinks, and converses during the performance. In such a setting, a brilliantly executed solo or a subtle delicate solo can sometimes fall upon deaf ears. Make sure you understand what will work best at the venue you are playing.

2. The Audience

How hip is the room? A more musically sophisticated audience presents the artist with greater freedom with regard to the employment of more highly evolved musical concepts during a solo. If the audience is mainly present for the purpose of partying, they will not show the level of interest or attention span required to receive and process a musically sophisticated solo. They should be fed a musical meal appropriate to their musical tastes at the moment.

3. The Show Premise (Entertainment, educational clinic, rock concert, etc.)

What is the focus of the event? Is it a celebration or an intimate and thoughtful musical performance event? Compare the show premise between a small, intimate jazz club in New York City that regularly showcases the best in straight-ahead jazz to that of the bigger than life stage of Madison Square Garden. Are you rocking the house? Rock your solo. Are you playing soothing jazz music? Keep that intensity and style in mind.

4. Timing

Does the solo occur during the first song in the set while the audience is only becoming acquainted with the artist and the surroundings, or later when a proper relationship has been created? Timing is everything. You're not going to light your guitar on fire for song 2 in the set. But at song 11, it might be just the right time.

5. The type of music being performed

Are you performing rap, R&B, country or acid jazz? Solos must be appropriate for not only the musical genre but also for the audience's level of musical sophistication and mood.

Share Your Emotions

For most musicians, the act of soloing is a very satisfying and enjoyable experience. During a solo, an artist runs through a gamut of emotions. As long as you are sharing your music, why not share your feelings as well. Try to picture some of your favorite musical artists who have allowed their feelings to show as they played. You could read the musical tension on the face of a guitar player as he bent the guitar string during a solo. You could see the intensity on the face of the violin player during a particularly difficult musical passage. Contrast that to a player who presented a deadpan or poker face during his performance. Ideally, it is preferable for an audience to experience not only a fantastic musical performance but also the personality and feelings of the performer during that performance. This adds an almost magical element to the show or concert.

Make it Personal

It is fairly common to see someone on stage playing a solo with their eyes closed or staring down at their shoes. One reason for this is that the act of creativity sometimes causes a person to mentally separate themselves from the audience in order to help them focus more easily. This is extremely unfortunate. Think about it. As the artist, you are there to perform for an audience. The lights are focused on you. You want them to be involved with you and your music. In the midst of all that you should not shut them out. "The eyes are the windows to the soul." When you close your eyes you shut the window. Yes, it is more difficult to personally present your musical efforts to an audience on a one-to-one basis, but it can be far more rewarding for your audience and for you also. You can close your eyes at points. Just don't linger there. Emote, engage, and perform. In reality, a show becomes much more compelling and engaging when the artist moves from one point of the stage to another during a solo, playing improvised phrases directly to individuals in the audience. As the artist, it forces you to assess whether or not the musical phrase is having an impact on that person.

For another thing, your movement on stage during the solo is visually more compelling to the audience resulting in greater attention being paid to your efforts. As a result of all this you become more than just a musician to them. You become more of a personality to them as well. They will get to know you better. By releasing your inhibitions and sharing each note and feeling with members of your audience you allow them to witness something that they might find difficult for themselves to do and they will appreciate you for that. You are injecting empathy into the experience.

CHAPTER TEN

RANDOM NOTES

WALKING OUT INTO THE AUDIENCE

Become familiar with the walkways and steps of the venue during the sound check. If you are inclined to go out into the audience for any reason whatsoever (to sing, play, or otherwise), it is highly recommended that you practice your steps once or twice before the show starts. This is an easy thing to do before, during, or after your sound check. Once you have some familiarity with the walkways and steps, you will be more confident about your walk, and you will find that fewer things go wrong.

When you are taking your practice walks out into the audience, try to find at least one alternative path back to the stage, even if one or more of the paths require you to go outside of the seating area and enter the stage from the back. You never know if during the show the audience is going to be crowding around rows or exits, impeding your mobility. You never know if security is going to block an entrance during a show too. As long as you have a good understanding of the room and you have a few options for returning to the stage, you should be okay.

It's good to get security, the stage manager and the front of house engineer "in the know" about when you're going to walk out into the audience. Security can make or break you, whether leading the way through the crowd or making sure the stage door is unlocked and open for you to return back to the stage from your journey into the audience. The sound engineer might have no idea that you're about to walk into the audience, and your mic will feed back once you walk in front of the PA. That's not good for anyone. So take a moment before the show to make sure you have your team in place so that your walk into the audience is successful and flawless.

As you can imagine, Murphy's Law really comes into play here (whatever can go wrong will go wrong AND at the worst possible moment). If you impulsively walk out into the audience motivated by adrenaline, without knowing the lay of the land, you may find that you're in quite a pickle. Just about anything can go wrong. You can even get hurt, or worse yet, hurt some unsuspecting fan. Some of the things that can go wrong are as follows:

- You may not see certain steps or levels in the floor, thereby hurting you and/or your instrument in the process of you falling.
- You may find that a section of your intended route may be roped off or blocked by crowding audience members.
- You may find that you still can't see anything once you get out into the audience, just as you couldn't see anything from the stage due to the bright lights. Or worse yet, you have a spotlight in your face following you, and blinding you every step of the way. Good luck on navigating your way.
- You may find that certain physical objects are more flimsy than they look close-up. For example, you may be tempted to jump on top of a ledge, wall or amplifier stack that may not be built to support your weight, or may not be stacked safely.

- Beware of timing issues as you walk or run around a theater or stadium. Sound only travels so fast. Count on being "off beat," depending on the venue, and a few rows out into the audience. Your band will be on stage and playing together. Meanwhile, you'll be walking or running around the audience playing to a delayed rhythm that you're hearing after the fact, due to sound traveling at a slow speed. In-ear monitors help this situation, but keep in mind that if you're just using stage monitors and the venue is large that you're playing, chances are you're going to have some slapback and/or a delay. You'll have to take that into consideration when playing.

As you can imagine, this is simply a short sample list. There are a number of other things that can go wrong when you're in such a vulnerable position. So plan well and carefully execute your plan!

JUMPING OR STAGE-DIVING INTO THE AUDIENCE

Jumping into the audience has become more and more popular in the last few decades. The movie *School of Rock* with Jack Black gives at least a few examples of the kinds of things that can go wrong if you try this! As it's easy to imagine what can go wrong when jumping into the audience, here are a few recommendations.

- Warn the audience either subtly or not so subtly that you might jump. Make eye contact. Make sure you have assurance, from some audience members, that they can and will catch you before you jump. Make sure that those audience members are capable of catching you and/or supporting you, not just a bunch of 100 lb. girls screaming for you.

- Spread your body out as much as you can. Make it easy for the people in the first few rows to grab you and support your weight. It is not inconceivable that you will find yourself sprawled on the floor (even when the crowd loves you). Once again, make it easy for people to catch you.
- It is assumed that anybody leaving the stage to mingle among the crowd will be connected wirelessly. If you have a microphone cable that connects your microphone or instrument to the sound system, do not leave the stage. Too much (potentially irreparable) damage can be done if you are dragging a microphone cable with you out into the audience.
- Do you have a cordless microphone with you? Don't under any circumstance hand it to an audience member. They'll either keep it as a memento, or sing or scream into it until security finds them and wrestles it from them. Don't drop it. It'll make a huge thud, and you'll never see it again. Hold on to it for dear life!
- Make sure you know your way back to the stage and have someone there to let you back in. Does security know you? Chances are they're not paying attention to you jumping off the stage. When you make your way back to the backstage entrance trying to get on stage after your leap of faith, you'll be asked for your backstage pass. Ugly. Have backup!! Or make sure the audience members that caught you in the first place can put you back (unlikely) or that you can climb back on your own.

GADGETS, TRICKS AND PYROTECHNICS

A few rules:

- Don't use too many gadgets and/or tricks. They may be thrilling for a moment; however, they can become boring (or old-hat) quickly if overused. Tricks in moderation work and can add to a show.

- Try your best to use gadgets and/or tricks at two strategic points in the show: <u>The beginning and the ending.</u> It's at these two points where audiences will most appreciate a thrill. Example: Fireworks at the end of a concert: Great!
- Try not to up-stage your own gadgets and/or tricks. You should make sure that the audience is looking at the appropriate location on the stage before the gadget or trick is used. You wouldn't want to cause any misdirection that would result in a large portion of the audience missing the excitement.

Pyrotechnics

It's obvious to note that the use of fire and explosives can be extremely dangerous to the band as well as the audience. The band Great White horrified the country with its pyrotechnics-gone-wrong that killed many people in the club. If you are going to use pyrotechnics, it is highly recommended that you hire seasoned professionals who will take all of the necessary precautionary measures to make sure everyone is (more than) safe from harm.

That being said, pyrotechnics can be an amazing part of a show. They are expensive, taking into consideration the safety precautions, the hiring of professionals, and the actual explosives, but they make a statement, and the biggest artists in the world use them to create a "wow" factor.

Examples of pyrotechnics:

1. "Sizzle Sticks" – One of the bands I toured with early on used tricks for each of its members to gain an audience response.

The best trick in my estimation was the one used by the drummer. He was called "Sizzle Sticks" throughout the show. Members of the audience wondered how he got his nickname and, close to the end of the show, he showed them. After a huge introduction, the front person introduced "Sizzle Sticks" at which time his drum tech lit his drumsticks on fire. He blew on them as if he were breathing fire, and played an entire drum solo with his sticks on fire. It was genius! Every night he received a standing ovation.

2. The German metal band Rammstein is historically a great live band. And they employ the use of pyro like no one else. On one tour, the two guitarists wore clear facemasks hooked up to gas tanks that they could blow gas through the mask to gain a torch effect. Richard Kruspe, one of the guitarists had this to say about the band's live pyrotechnics. "You have to understand that 99 percent of the people don't understand the lyrics, so you have to come up with something to keep the drama in the show. We have to do something. We like to have a show; we like to play with fire. We do have a sense of humor. We do laugh about it; we have fun… but we're not Spinal Tap. We take the music and the lyrics seriously."

A Fun Story

"When I co-wrote "Eye Of The Tiger" for Rocky 3, my group Survivor had a 10 million dollar video to help promote it, but when we went out on the road, we were on our own without a net. And this song was the capper of the set. It had to be spectacular. The lights would dim and suddenly from the darkness came my now iconic telegraphic 16th note muted guitar figure followed by a state of the art recording of the backward cymbal and piano whooooosh! Then the slashing chords as the vari lights went crazy and smoke filled the stage. Dave was singing not only to the front row of rabid fans but also to the back row. That's the kind of emotional projection and sense of purpose you need to connect with a house of 20,000. By the end of the song, guitarist Frankie Sullivan was up in the rafters with his wireless guitars defying space and gravity. So effects meet emotion, and chaos ensues. Today with my current band The Ides of March, we play without the smoke bombs and flash pots. As fun as it was to have all the onstage tricks working for you, I have always said that the greatest special effect is human connection."

> —**Jim Peterik**, co-founder of The Ides of March and Survivor. Writer of "Eye Of The Tiger," "Vehicle," and 18 top 20 hits. Author of "Songwriting For Dummies" and veteran of Madison Square Garden

"THE SHOW MUST GO ON," AND OTHER SHOW BIZ SLOGANS

Performers have numerous luxuries. They work in an environment that most people envy. They do what they love and get paid for it. At the same time, there are some show business codes regarding what is expected of anyone who calls himself a professional entertainer. Here are a few:

1. **"The Show Must Go On"**
2. **"There are no Excuses"**
3. **"It's Never the Audience's Fault"**
4. **"You're Only as Good as your worst Show."**

These truths are exemplified by the following stories:

What Happens When You're Sick?

In 1970, a much-revered older show group that dated all the way back to the days of vaudeville, was playing one of the top hotel showrooms in North Miami Beach. Their shows were a master class in how to meet and please an audience. They knew how to turn a nightclub audience into a major party. During one particular night, something odd was happening. At several points during the show, one of the front men would be missing onstage. A short while later he would always reappear with a big smile and giving his all. Sitting out in the audience a friend of the group was curious as to what was wrong.

After the show, he went backstage and asked one of the group members why the front person had left the stage. He was told that he had a severe case of the flu, and that he was running offstage to throw up into a bucket. After completing this, he'd run back out on stage and continue performing. Not one person in the audience could have detected that he was ill that night. He never would have allowed it to show because he was a professional.

The moral of the story is: "A true professional never allows the show to suffer for <u>any</u> reason."

CARDINAL RULE:
You're only as good as your worst show.

It's so easy to do a great show for a full house of hundreds or thousands of adoring people, but what if the venue draws an alarmingly small crowd? You cannot blame a mediocre show on the fact that the audience was simply too small. Never allow the size of the audience to affect the energy and quality of the show. Most experienced entertainers have found themselves in this situation. Disappointment and the feeling of potential failure fills the air. People scattered here and there throughout the room are waiting for any excuse to get up and leave. Nobody has high expectations. After all, would a performer really give his all to such a small crowd?

The psychology behind performing to a small crowd is this: The audience in a town will notice if your show is not well attended. The people who hear of the low turnout will wonder, "What went wrong? Is there a problem with the performers? Are there any other problems?" If you go out on stage and do the least amount possible simply to comply with the mandates of the contract, then the answer will be clear. The performers really aren't all that good and the people were correct to stay away from the venue. On the other hand, if the performers execute an excellent, even amazing show for the very small audience, then the opposite will become clear. The people made a mistake by not attending the show. Although the promoter may decide not to bring the entertainers back, there is a small chance the promoter will try once again since the first perform-ance was amazingly good. In addition, people from this town may decide to travel to another town in order to see what they missed. Or they'll tell their friends how great your show was, so more people will attend next time. This is certainly making the most of a disappointing situation. Always make the most of a bad situation.

You Never Know

The following is a story told by a head maitre d' at one of the biggest hotels in Las Vegas. The time period was around 1969. It was the last show of the night during the graveyard shift, 3:00 AM in the morning. The room was a 600-seat theater that presented up-and-coming acts at the time such as Ike and Tina Turner, Redd Foxx, and Frankie Laine. The entire room was empty except for two tables containing a total of nine people. The scheduled performer peered through the edge of the stage curtains to check out the house, saw the mostly empty room and then positioned himself onstage for the opening of his show. As soon as the curtains were opened and the lights came up, the entertainer strode out on stage and gave a stellar performance on the opening song. He finished his opening number, and then told the nine people that, although the audience was very small, it would have absolutely no effect on the magnitude of the party that they were about to experience. From that point onward, he did the entire show as if it were to a sold-out room.

There was a mystery guest in the room that night. Throughout the show, the performer noticed the dark silhouette of someone sitting in the back of the room, but he never got a good, clear look at the person. Once his performance was over and the audience showed their appreciation, the performer went back to the dressing room to change. All of sudden there came a knock at the door. The maitre d' informed the performer that a highly successful star in Las Vegas had been sitting in the back of the room and had stayed throughout the entire show. This star asked if he could come up to the dressing room and meet the performer. Of course, the answer was "Yes." The star came into the dressing and told the performer that he was overwhelmed with the fact that the size of the audience had no effect on the quality of the show. He felt he had witnessed a true professional at work. Because of this, he offered the performer an opening spot in the main room of the hotel he was playing. Our performer's life and career were elevated forever. The moral to the story is, "You never know who is watching you."

Consider the following suggestions:

1. When the crowd is small and the room feels intimate, invite everyone to take seats in the front and center. Suggest this idea very positively without being forceful or negative in any way. Some may take you up on the invitation, and some may not. If most of the people accept the invitation and sit in the first few rows, the show can be a great deal of fun, as it will be easier to interact with everyone.

2. You never know who might be attending your show, so always be in the best possible form. No excuses. Consistency is everything, and the people coming to see you at a tiny club in your small home town should enjoy the same excellence as the thousands watching you at Coachella.

3. Let's say the audience is tiny and unresponsive, or you have a bad case of the flu. Maybe your dog just died. Everything is working against you. To what degree can you allow this to negatively impact your performance? The best performers will carry on in spite of the worst circumstances. They may fall apart backstage after the show, but they will never allow it to affect the quality of performance that they give to their audience.

SELF IMPROVEMENT

Learn How to Critique Yourself

Videotape your performances. Place a camera in the audience and focus it on yourself. Hand your phone to a friend in the club. Have them film you. Review the video afterwards. Video does not lie. Put yourself in the position of an audience member and ask yourself if that person on stage (you) is:

- Executing the parts perfectly?
- Communicating with members of the audience?
- Reaching out into the audience to build relationships?
- Working hard on stage?
- Accessible and likeable as a person?
- Accepting applause sincerely?
- Performing a well-paced show?
- Preventing dreaded dead air?

Become a Student of Exceptional Stage Performance

Whenever you hear about a performer or a group that has a solid reputation, go see them in action, even if they specialize in another genre. Try to determine what things are working for them. If any of these things would be applicable for you, work them into your onstage world! Just as musicians "steal" musical licks, you can steal performance licks. Add new ideas that will work successfully for you and throw away the ones that don't. The world of entertainment is your classroom and all you need to do is go to class. Study everyone. Even some of the worst acts might have one thing you can use to improve your own live performance.

CHAPTER ELEVEN

WHEN THINGS GO WRONG

IF ANYTHING CAN GO WRONG, IT WILL GO WRONG AT THE WORST POSSIBLE MOMENT (MURPHY'S LAW)

ABAIR'S COMMENTARY ON MURPHY'S LAW:
"MURPHY WAS AN OPTIMIST"

There are two major categories of mistakes that can happen on stage.

1. Obvious
2. Not obvious

Regardless of how much of a professional you might be, things can and do go wrong from time to time. What could happen?

- A guitar string breaks
- A microphone stops working
- The lead singer forgets the lyrics
- A drum head breaks
- Somebody trips and falls
- The power goes out
- A group member gets sick
- It starts to rain (when you're outdoors)
- A member of the audience heckles you
- You play something incorrectly
- Your background tracks skip or play at the wrong time

No matter what happens, you must take the appropriate steps to solve the problem with **grace and dignity.**

Take stock of any situation, and take care of the problem as quickly and painlessly as possible. Once everything is repaired, the entire situation will be forgotten soon enough, and the show will go on. Don't draw unnecessary attention to it through overly trying to cover it up!

In many instances, most people will never know that a problem has occurred. You can assume most of the audience has never seen the show before, so they have nothing to compare it with. They might even think any problem (sour note, forgotten line, blown fuse) was planned! Once the performers get past these gaffes, the audience rarely knows the difference, much less remembers it. Even experts are frequently fooled. In most cases, the audience will be totally unaware anything bad happened unless it is specifically called to their attention.

When a gaffe occurs, no matter how bad, do your best to look as if everything is going along smoothly and as planned. Do not let your facial expressions telegraph the fact that something is wrong. Fix the problem and move on. If it is impossible for the audience not to have noticed, acknowledge the problem and get back to the show as quickly as possible. Don't dwell on it or get caught up in explaining what happened.

Here are a couple of examples of well-handled and not-so-well-handled mishaps.

- **Head over heels**

   One night I was on stage rocking out, and having a great time. We were in the zone and playing our hearts out.

As I was strutting across the stage, I tripped, caught my foot on a guitar cable, and flew backwards into the guitar amplifier. Luckily, the band was in tune with what was going on, and so the guitar player quickly reached out his hand and caught me. Obviously, the entire audience saw what happened. There was no "cover up" that would make it seem like it never happened. I took a melodramatic bow to the audience and lifted my arm towards the band member who saved me in recognition and honor, again with much melodrama. The audience roared. I bought him a drink later in honor of saving my life!

• **Don't blow your fuse**

Halfway through a song on stage, a fuse of an amplifier blew for a friend of mine who plays guitar. He decided to fix the problem while trying his best to limit any disruption to the show. He put his guitar on its stand and went behind his amplifier to find the blown fuse. Once he found the fuse, he crawled on his hands and knees (in plain view of the audience) to the side of the stage. Obviously, the entire audience no longer paid any attention to the band. Their eyes were GLUED to the guy on his hands and knees! This significant act of misdirection was comical to say the least. As the guy came back, once again on his hands and knees, to insert the new fuse, the audience cheered sarcastically. At this point, the guitar player put his guitar back on and started playing as if nothing had happened. It would have been far better to have put the guitar down, popped out the fuse, run off stage to get a new one, popped in the new one, and then carry on. There was no reason to try to hide this unfortunate circumstance from the audience. Obviously, the fuse had to be replaced in order to go on with a good show.

- **Ashlee Simpson dances a jig on Saturday Night Live**

  One of the most well-known stage errors happened live on the TV show Saturday Night Live with a well-known female pop singer Ashlee Simpson, whose band was playing one song and the pre-recorded vocal track was playing another song. The problem originated with her attempt to lip-sync when she was supposed to be singing live. Such an unfortunate turn of events cannot be ignored since it was witnessed by almost everyone in the audience. The singer's response to the problem was to do a jig and walk off stage. While this is a complicated situation, there are things she could have done differently that could have saved the day for her. What would have been a better fix than her jig?

  She could have turned around to whoever was running her background tracks and told him to cut the tracks. From there, she could continue with the song they were in the middle of playing, minus the errant background tracks. It would be her and the band without any background help, but the live broadcast wouldn't be a total loss.

  Know what's happening around you, react constantly to it, and interact with your band to create good out of a bad situation. She was a new artist, and she was still developing her knowledge of how to perform. She learned a valuable lesson that day. It was unfortunate that it had to be in front of millions of people.

- **Ray Charles vs. Eugene 'Big Bubba' Ross**

  In 1983 one of the most famous on stage altercations occurred between Ray Charles and guitarist Eugene 'Big Bubba' Ross. It seems Eugene Ross was more and more unhappy with tour conditions. He was uncomfortable on the bus, due to his wooden leg and long travel distances, and he complained that the tour never stopped long enough for a proper meal. He was angry that Ray Charles was making millions while his band was still scraping by. So night after night the tension grew between Eugene Ross and Ray Charles on stage. Eugene was too loud night after night, and the engineer and Ray would complain to him. Finally, in 1983 Ray Charles thought he was too loud on stage and told him to "Cut it out." Eugene 'Big Bubba' Ross started screaming that he was a dog on stage, and Ray Charles had him taken off the stage in the middle of a song as graciously as possible saying "I love this man. God bless him. Get him off the stage."

- **Singing in the rain**

  One evening, a jazz concert was being held in a beautiful out-door amphitheater. About two songs into the show, it began to rain. It wasn't a light rain. It was a downpour! Everyone ran indoors and assumed the show was cancelled. The artist on stage ran indoors alongside the audience members, and herded them into the lobby of the hotel next door to the amphitheater. He put on an hour show for the remaining audience with the piano in the hotel lobby to the delight of everyone. I bet everyone bought a ticket to his next show because of his graciousness that night.

- **A memorable Memorial Day**

  One evening an artist was scheduled to play a huge festival on Memorial Day. It was a slightly long drive to get there, but it was very doable. All of the band members were stuck in extreme traffic due to the holiday, but most arrived on time.

The guitarist in the band hadn't taken into account the possibility of this extreme traffic and was still on the road when show time arrived. When it was time to take the stage, the artist had two choices.

A. They could go on stage without a guitarist and try to get through as many songs as possible that didn't feature guitar. Or,

B. They could grab the co-writer/producer who happened to be in the audience that day and bring him on stage to play the first few songs to "fill in" for their late guitarist until he arrived.

They chose B because it allowed the artist to portray the producer and co-writer coming on stage as something special...a gift to the audience that didn't happen very often. It made them feel as if they were getting to see some "behind the scenes" insight that not every audience got to see. In reality, he was filling in and saving the show! The regular guitarist showed up during the third song and stealthily tuned his guitar and got ready for the switcheroo. The producer was thanked for "sitting in" and the regular guitarist finally joined the concert. The audience loved it, and even commented afterwards how special they thought that was to feature the producer on stage. He signed autographs afterwards! They turned lemons into lemonade!

HOW TO HANDLE HECKLERS

In Chapter Two the importance of keeping control of your show was discussed. No matter what happens, **control is paramount**. From time to time, a person from the audience will try to take control of the show by heckling. Sometimes heckling takes the form of an audience member saying rude things loudly enough for others to hear and be distracted by. At other times, an audience member may engage in some damaging or humiliating activity in an attempt to attract attention. At other times, the audience member is trying to have a conversation with the artist and/or have their voice heard. In any of these situations, it's important to keep your cool and <u>stay in control of your show.</u>

"An ounce of prevention is worth a pound of cure."
—Benjamin Franklin

The best way to prevent heckling is to make sure that the show pressure is high. Exercise proper show flow by intelligently using applause cycles to ensure that something is always happening (music, solos, talking to the audience, etc.). If something compelling is always happening, there is simply no time for an audience member to call attention to him/herself. Don't allow a moment of "dead air" to provide a platform for a heckler.

This being said, no matter how high you keep the pressure on the audience or how streamlined your show is, there are going to be points in the show that people will yell things out at you like "I love you" or play "Song X." Feel free to answer those people. Tell them "I love you" back. Or say "By request, I'm going to play a song for that man in the fourth row who just asked for it." So how do you know when to and when not to respond to these types of outbursts? Learn to read intentions of people. Is the outburst in tune with the show? Is the audience member feeding off what you are giving him/her and just being vocal about it? If the outburst is short, sweet and well intentioned, then respond to it.

On the other hand, if someone starts talking to hear him/herself talk or to take the attention away from the show, you should not respond. You should go on with the show. The rule of thumb is to ignore them and hope they run out of energy (or drugs/ alcohol) and simply stop. If they stop, there is no significant damage done. If they don't stop, here are a couple of suggestions to help you deal with the heckler:

- Send a subtle request to your group manager and/or security to appropriately handle the situation.
- Politely ask people seated in close proximity to the heckler to, "Please help the poor guy out." Don't communicate with the heckler directly. Only ask the people around the heckler to help you. In most cases, the people around the heckler will be so embarrassed that they will find a way to "shush" him/her up.

A Quick Story

A talented comic was performing in a small club. He seemed good and had established a good rapport with the audience. All of a sudden, a heckler started shouting in an obnoxious manner. Instead of the comic asking for people to help the poor guy, he started a dialog with him. The dialog went as follows:

Heckler: "Can I ask you a question?"

Comic: After a pause, "Sure..."

Heckler: "How do you keep an idiot in suspense?"

Comic: After thinking for a few moments, "Hm-m-m.... I don't know. How?" A few more moments went by. "I really don't know... OK. Please tell me how." More time went by...

The audience started laughing, as they finally understood the joke. The heckler **proved** that he was funny and all eyes were on him. The comic had now been cleverly called an idiot with impunity. Unfortunately for the comedian, there was no way to recover. Don't gamble with such a loose cannon.

Exception: Some comics actually build a show around encouraging people to heckle from the audience. Their act is built on brilliant and humorous responses to heckler's remarks. These comics are typically very bright, witty, and very experienced. Such a show can be hilarious as long as the comic can stay in control. Don't try this unless you're really experienced and ready for the challenge.

A Two-Part Story About a Heckler

Part 1

A few years ago, a band with a very dynamic front person was performing in Dallas. In the middle of a show, someone in the audience started heckling. The front person tried to ignore him but he wouldn't stop. Finally, after the front person had reached the end of his patience, he stopped the show and began telling the following story to the audience:

"Once, when I was very young, I was visiting my grandparents on their farm. My grandfather asked me to help move some hay bales into the hayloft of his barn. The procedure required the assistance of his old mule. The process involved tying a rope wrapped around a hay bale on the ground to a rope connected to a block and tackle just above the open door of the hayloft at the top of the barn. The other end of the rope would be tied to the old mule who was supposed to begin moving, thus causing the hay bale to rise up to the level of the upper door at which point I could swing the hay into the hayloft. *Meanwhile the audience was listening intently with much curiosity. People love stories.*

Unfortunately, the old mule refused to cooperate. It stood its ground defiantly in spite of all my shouting and pleading. I tried kicking him and whipping him with a stick. Finally, when I reached my wit's end I pulled out a pitchfork and started stabbing the mule to get it to move, but unfortunately I went a little too far and, before I realized it, the mule was lying on the ground dead. *At this point the audience is completely sucked in.*

When my grandfather realized what had happened he shook his finger at me and said, "Shame on you for killing that old mule! Someday that jackass is going to come back and haunt you!" and I never believed him until tonight!" AND THE FRONT PERSON POINTED OUT INTO THE AUDIENCE DIRECTLY AT THE HECKLER! The audience busted out laughing at the heckler, humiliating him.

Part 2: And now, for the rest of the story . . .
Following the show, the band was seated in the dressing room when, all of a sudden, the manager of the club walked in with a worried look on his face. He said, "We've got to get you (the front person) out of here right now! Apparently, the person doing the heckling was out on bail for shooting somebody with a shotgun, and had told members of the audience seated around him that he was going to kill the front person for humiliating him. Needless to say, he was sneaked out the back door of the club averting a potential disaster.

The moral of this story is to let the management or security of the venue deal with hecklers, unless they are a deliberate part of your act.

CHAPTER TWELVE

FINAL THOUGHTS

THIS IS NO DRESS REHEARSAL, WE <u>ARE</u> PROFESSIONALS AND THIS <u>IS</u> THE BIG TIME!

THE TRUTH

If you're going to make the decision to stand on a stage, in any genre of music or performance, under the brilliant lights, with a professional sound system properly equalized to perfection, you had better do everything within your power to please the crowd. They wouldn't be there in the first place unless their expectations were high. You are "on the spot." You must take control and lead the crowd on a journey they will not soon forget. You need every edge you can get to make your performance great. If you don't make the most of your performance, they will abandon you for the next act that comes their way. You must make a big and emphatic statement when you have the stage. You must make your mark, and you have little time to do it.

Imagine that you are sitting in the audience of a Rolling Stones concert and Mick Jagger walks offstage into the audience, and walks directly up to your seat. With a friendly smile on his face, he tells you how happy he is to meet you, and that he hopes you're enjoying the show. Once back on stage, Mick continues to acknowledge you visually to ensure that you are having a great time. How would that make you feel by the end of the show? Do you think you would become a bigger fan? Of course you would. It is this kind of feeling that you should leave with every member of your audience. This is in essence what Mick Jagger is doing from the stage. He's thanking you by looking into your eyes and singing to you and celebrating with you with every gesture he makes.

It's not all about the music. It's about people and what they like and what they respond to. Musicians should work hard to develop the ability to visually give of themselves as they play. You should not only be focused on providing a first-class musical performance but also on connecting with and pleasing your audiences. By building friendships from the stage you are building a devoted customer base. After your shows, your fans will go out and tell other people about the performer(s) who created a magical journey of music through the use of surprises, creative hills and valleys, humor, and a bond of communication. They don't know or use these terms, but they know they had a great time. People always want to experience such a journey over and over.

Every time you return to play a certain locale you will be greeted by ever-increasing numbers of devoted fans that feel as if they know you and like you. There is no greater feeling than doing what you love the most in front of an eager and appreciative audience.

In conclusion, we, the writers of this book, wish to thank you, the readers of this book, for taking the time and initiative to give yourself an edge and work toward being the best performer you can be. We appreciate you and applaud you!!

Now, go out there and get those standing ovations!
You know How To Play Madison Square Garden.

GLOSSARY OF TERMS

Pressure – The process of taking the audience to a state of anxious anticipation. A state when the performer(s) are in control of the audience's attention. The compelling force or influence a performance has on an audience.

Dead Air – Any point in the show where no one is in control and/or nothing is happening.

The 100% Rule – Do and say things that work 100% of the time.

Misdirection – When someone upstages another person on stage. The act of, either consciously or unconsciously, directing the audience's attention away from something happening on stage.

Hills and Valleys – The up-and-down flow of a show with respect to energy and intensity. The ebb-and-flow of the features or intensity of a performance.

Front Person – The primary focal point person on stage.

Side Man – A backup musician or member of the band other than the front person.

Working The Crowd – Maintaining an entertaining and controlling presence with the audience. This is used to maintain or increase pressure.

Trashcan Ending – A massive, long lasting, dramatic last chord to a song.

Hook – Any part of a performance that is memorable and compelling enough that most people can understand and therefore be attracted to it over and over.

Mystique – The "It" factor that separates performers from the typical man on the street.

Stage Presence – That which a performer possesses, and actively uses on stage to attract and retain the attention of an audience.

Mindi Abair

Mindi Abair is a saxophonist, singer, composer, author and radio show host.

As a solo artist, she has produced ten #1 radio singles and five major label solo releases for Verve and Concord Records that have topped the Contemporary Jazz Charts, "It Just Happens That Way" (2003), "Come As You Are" (2004), "Life Less Ordinary" (2006), "Stars" (2008), and "In Hi Fi Stereo" (2010).

Mindi hosts the internationally syndicated radio show "Chill With Mindi Abair," and she is a staff writer for Wine and Jazz magazine, penning her own column "Wine and Jazz With a Star." She is a Berklee College of Music graduate, an elected governor for the Los Angeles Chapter of NARAS, and an Artist Ambassador for Campell's Labels for Education and The Grammy Foundation. Mindi was featured on the 2011 season of "American Idol" as a soloist with Paul McDonald and Casey Abrams, won Best International Instrumentalist at the 2011 Wave Awards in Toronto, and Best Female Artist of the Year at the 2011 Oasis Contemporary Jazz Awards. She also appeared on the 2011 season for the Fran Drescher show "Happily Divorced."

The list of artists she has toured or recorded with are a testament to her talent. They include Keb' Mo', Lalah Hathaway, Duran Duran, Lee Ritenour, the Backstreet Boys, Mandy Moore, Max Weinberg, Bill Champlin, David Pack, Mocean Worker, Adam Sandler, Rick Braun, Teena Marie, Bobby Lyle, Jonathan Butler, and Peter White. Mindi's website is: www.mindiabair.com

Lance Abair

Lance Abair, a music producer, entertainment coach and multi-instrumentalist, started writing songs on the piano at the age of four, began saxophone at the age of fourteen and almost immediately started performing in local bands. He toured the United States for five years playing saxophone and keyboards in a highly successful comedy/show band "The Fabulous Entertainers."

The next eleven years he spent as the talent coordinator and entertainment coach for Young American Showcase, a Florida-based musical touring company where, each year, young rock musicians from all over the U.S. were taught and rehearsed on all of the basic entertainment concepts. After rehearsal camp, they were assembled into eight rock bands to tour throughout the entire school year, under the names of "Free Fare" and "Freedom Jam," playing assemblies and night concerts in junior and senior high schools throughout the U.S. and Canada.

Lance later toured for three years playing saxophone and keyboards with Mark Farner from Grand Funk Railroad. He has held the positions of Senior Product Specialist for KORG, Product Manager and Artist Relations for Clavia, and Senior Trainer, Pro Products, for Bose Corporation. He is also a well-known writer, producer and video host of internationally distributed instructional videos from Mark of the Unicorn's Performer to KORG Keyboard Workstations.

Ross Cooper
At the age of 17, Ross Cooper joined Young American Showcase and played guitar touring across the United States performing about 200 shows per year for the next 6 years.

Leaving music behind after his early years of touring, Ross now has 25 years of experience as a software developer and entrepreneur. He is an inventor with numerous patents to his name. He is also the author of a software program named "The Preparation for the SAT" which has sold over one million units in the U.S.A. Since 1984, Ross has been responsible for the creation and operation of numerous start-up technology companies in the areas of Psychometrics, Health Sciences, Telecommunications and Digital Television Distribution. In the year 2000,

Mr. Cooper founded the company Verimatrix, which is a recognized leader in content security and watermarking. In 2008, Mr. Cooper founded Channel Islands, a pioneer in targeted advertising systems for television.

For more information about this book,
contact the authors at:
www.howtoplaymadisonsquaregarden.com

CPSIA information can be obtained at www.ICGtesting.com
Printed in the USA
LVOW06s0027020114

367618LV00008BA/1021/P

9 780983 936305